Here and Now

HENRI J.M. NOUWEN

Here and Now

LIVING IN THE SPIRIT

with Guide for Reflection

A Crossroad Book
The Crossroad Publishing Company
New York

The Crossroad Publishing Company
481 Eighth Avenue, New York, NY 10001

Copyright © 1994 by Henri J. M. Nouwen

"Guide for Reflection" copyright © 2003 by
The Crossroad Publishing Company

Printed in the United States of America

Library of Congress Cataloging-in-Publication Data

Nouwen, Henri J. M.
    Here and now : living in the Spirit / Henri J.M. Nouwen.
    p. cm.
    ISBN 0-8245-1409-2 (cloth) ; ISBN 0-8245-1967-1 (pbk.)
    1. Spiritual life – Catholic Church – Meditations. 2. Nouwen, Henri J. M.
I. Title.
BX2182.2.N668   1994
248.4′82 – dc20   94-20895

3   4   5   6   7   8   9   10   06   05   04   03

Contents

Contents

Acknowledgments

Three friends have helped me very much in the preparation of this book: Kathy Christie, who typed and retyped the manuscript in many ways and forms, Conrad Wieczorek, who spent much time editing the text, and Bob Heller, who chose the themes and gave the book its final structure. I am deeply grateful for their competence, kindness, and generosity.

Special thanks go to Peggy McDonnell, her family, and friends, who, in memory of Murray McDonnell, offered me all the necessary support to find the time and place to write these meditations.

Finally I want to express my deep gratitude to Bart and Patricia Gavigan and to Franz and Reny Johna for always offering me a safe home away from home.

Preface

One day I simply sat down behind my desk and began to write down thoughts and feelings that emerged from my mind and heart. Except for the Bible, I had no other books to quote from. Once I had started I was surprised how easy it was to keep writing. It seemed as if each thought called forth another thought and each feeling gave birth to another feeling. It became a long examination of conscience, an extended personal statement of faith, and a series of glimpses into the kingdom of God. I found I was writing about myself, my friends and family, and my God, all connected in many intricate ways.

Much of what I have written has been part of my life for as long as I can remember, much too, has come to my spiritual awareness during the last few years, and much appeared as new and surprising as I wrote these meditations. I didn't try to be original, but to be authentic. I didn't try to say things I had never said before, but things that really matter to me. I didn't try to write a new book, but to meditate on life as I am trying to live it. Some of the reflections in this book can also be found in earlier books; others are new. But all are an expression of my present state of mind and heart.

The various meditations in this book stand on their own. They can be read independently of each other. Still I have tried to weave the different meditations around some larger themes, so that when read together, a coherent vision of the spiritual life becomes visible. It is like a mosaic: each little stone has a unique significance, but together, and seen from a certain distance, they show something new that each individual stone cannot show.

I hope and pray that you who read these meditations will discover many connections with your own spiritual journey, even when that journey is very different from my own. I trust that these connections will make you aware that we are traveling together toward the Light, always encouraging each other to keep our eyes fixed on the One who is calling us home.

Chapter I

LIVING IN
THE PRESENT

One: A New Beginning

A new beginning! We must learn to live each day, each hour, yes, each minute as a new beginning, as a unique opportunity to make everything new. Imagine that we could live each moment as a moment pregnant with new life. Imagine that we could live each day as a day full of promises. Imagine that we could walk through the new year always listening to a voice saying to us: "I have a gift for you and can't wait for you to see it!" Imagine.

Is it possible that our imagination can lead us to the truth of our lives? Yes, it can! The problem is that we allow our past, which becomes longer and longer each year, to say to us: "You know it all; you have seen it all, be realistic; the future will be just another repeat of the past. Try to survive it as best you can." There are many cunning foxes jumping on our shoulders and whispering in our ears the great lie: "There is nothing new under the sun . . . don't let yourself be fooled."

When we listen to these foxes, they eventually prove themselves right: our new year, our new day, our new hour become flat, boring, dull, and without anything new.

So what are we to do? First, we must send the foxes back to where they belong: in their foxholes. And then we must open our minds and our hearts to the voice that resounds through the valleys and hills of our life saying: "Let me show you where I live among my people. My name is 'God-with-you.' I will wipe away all the tears from your eyes; there will be no more death, and no more mourning or sadness. The world of the past has gone" (see Revelation 21:2–5).

We must choose to listen to that voice, and every choice will open us a little more to discover the new life hidden in the moment, waiting eagerly to be born.

Two: Without "Oughts" and "Ifs"

It is hard to live in the present. The past and the future keep harassing us. The past with guilt, the future with worries. So many things have happened in our lives about which we feel uneasy, regretful, angry, confused, or, at least, ambivalent. And all these feelings are often colored by guilt. Guilt that says: "You ought to have done something other than what you did; you ought to have said something other than what you said." These "oughts" keep us feeling guilty about the past and prevent us from being fully present to the moment.

Worse, however, than our guilt are our worries. Our worries fill our lives with "What ifs": "What if I lose my job, what if my father dies, what if there is not enough money, what if the economy goes down, what if a war breaks out?" These many "ifs" can so fill our mind that we become blind to the flowers in the garden and the smiling children on the streets, or deaf to the grateful voice of a friend.

The real enemies of our life are the "oughts" and the "ifs." They pull us backward into the unalterable past and forward into the unpredictable future. But real life takes place in the here and the now. God is a God of the present. God is always in the moment, be that moment hard or easy, joyful or painful. When Jesus spoke about God, he always spoke about God as being where and when we are. "When you see me,

you see God. When you hear me you hear God."
God is not someone who was or will be, but the One
who is, and who is for me in the present moment.
That's why Jesus came to wipe away the burden of
the past and the worries for the future. He wants us
to discover God right where we are, here and now.

Three: Birthdays

Birthdays need to be celebrated. I think it is more
important to celebrate a birthday than a successful
exam, a promotion, or a victory. Because to celebrate a birthday means to say to someone: "Thank
you for being you." Celebrating a birthday is exalt-
ing life and being glad for it. On a birthday we do not
say: "Thanks for what you did, or said, or accom-
plished." No, we say: "Thank you for being born
and being among us."

On birthdays we celebrate the present. We do not
complain about what happened or speculate about
what will happen, but we lift someone up and let
everyone say: "We love you."

I know a friend who, on his birthday, is picked up
by his friends, carried to the bathroom, and thrown

clothes and all into a tub full of water. Everyone eagerly awaits his birthday, even he himself. I have no idea where this tradition came from, but to be lifted up and "re-baptized" seems like a very good way to have your life celebrated. We are made aware that although we have to keep our feet on the ground, we are created to reach to the heavens, and that, although we easily get dirty, we can always be washed clean again and our life given a new start.

Celebrating a birthday reminds us of the goodness of life, and in this spirit we really need to celebrate people's birthdays every day, by showing gratitude, kindness, forgiveness, gentleness, and affection. These are ways of saying: "It's good that you are alive; it's good that you are walking with me on this earth. Let's be glad and rejoice. This is the day that God has made for us to be and to be together."

Four: Here and Now

To live in the present, we must believe deeply that what is most important is the here and the now. We are constantly distracted by things that have happened in the past or that might happen in the future.

It is not easy to remain focused on the present. Our mind is hard to master and keeps pulling us away from the moment.

Prayer is the discipline of the moment. When we pray, we enter into the presence of God whose name is God-with-us. To pray is to listen attentively to the One who addresses us here and now. When we dare to trust that we are never alone but that God is always with us, always cares for us, and always speaks to us, then we can gradually detach ourselves from the voices that make us guilty or anxious and thus allow ourselves to dwell in the present moment. This is a very hard challenge because radical trust in God is not obvious. Most of us distrust God. Most of us think of God as a fearful, punitive authority or as an empty, powerless nothing. Jesus' core message was that God is neither a powerless weakling nor a powerful boss, but a lover, whose only desire is to give us what our hearts most desire.

To pray is to listen to that voice of love. That is what obedience is all about. The word "obedience" comes from the Latin word *ob-audire,* which means to listen with great attentiveness. Without listening, we become "deaf" to the voice of love. The Latin word for deaf is *surdus*. To be completely deaf is to be *absurdus,* yes, absurd. When we no longer pray, no longer listen to the voice of love that speaks to us in the moment, our lives become absurd lives in which we are thrown back and forth between the past and the future.

If we could just be, for a few minutes each day, fully where we are, we would indeed discover that we are not alone and that the One who is with us wants only one thing: to give us love.

Five: Our Inner Room

Listening to the voice of love requires that we direct our minds and hearts toward that voice with all our attention. How can we do that? The most fruitful way — in my experience — is to take a simple prayer, a sentence or a word, and slowly repeat it. We can use the Lord's Prayer, the Jesus Prayer, the name of Jesus, or any word that reminds us of God's love and put it in the center of our inner room, like a candle in a dark space.

Obviously we will be constantly distracted. We will think about what happened yesterday or what will happen tomorrow. We will have long, imaginary discussions with our friends or enemies. We will plan our next day, prepare our upcoming talk, or organize our next meeting. Still, as long as we keep the candle in our dark room burning, we can return to that light and see clearly the presence of the One who offers us what we most desire.

This is not always a satisfying experience. Often we are so restless and so unable to find inner quietude that we can't wait to get busy again, thus avoiding the confrontation with the chaotic state of our minds and hearts. Still, when we remain faithful to our discipline, even if it is only ten minutes a day, we gradually come to see — by the candlelight of our prayers — that there is a space within us where God dwells and where we are invited to dwell with God. Once we come to know that inner, holy place, a place more beautiful and precious than any place we can travel to, we want to be there and be spiritually fed.

Six: With Others

One of the discoveries we make in prayer is that the closer we come to God, the closer we come to all our brothers and sisters in the human family. God is not a private God. The God who dwells in our inner sanctuary is also the God who dwells in the inner sanctuary of each human being. As we recognize God's presence in our own hearts, we can also recognize that presence in the hearts of others, because the God who has chosen us as a dwelling-place gives us the eyes to see the God who dwells in others. When we see only demons within ourselves, we can see only demons in others, but when we see God within ourselves, we can see God also in others.

This might sound rather theoretical, but when we pray, we will increasingly experience ourselves as part of a human family infinitely bound by God who created us to share, all of us, in the divine light.

We often wonder what we can do for others, especially for those in great need. It is not a sign of powerlessness when we say: "We must pray for one another." To pray for one another is, first of all, to acknowledge, in the presence of God, that we belong to each other as children of the same God. Without this acknowledgment of human solidarity, what we do for one another does not flow from who we truly are. We are brothers and sisters, not competitors or rivals. We are children of one God, not partisans of different gods.

To pray, that is, to listen to the voice of the One who calls us the "beloved," is to learn that that voice excludes no one. Where I dwell, God dwells with me and where God dwells with me I find all my sisters and brothers. And so intimacy with God and solidarity with all people are two aspects of dwelling in the present moment that can never be separated.

Seven: The Hub of Life

In my home country, the Netherlands, you still see many large wagon wheels, not on wagons, but as decorations at the entrances of farms or on the walls of restaurants. I have always been fascinated by these wagon wheels: with their wide rims, strong wooden spokes, and big hubs. These wheels help me to understand the importance of a life lived from the center. When I move along the rim, I can reach one spoke after the other, but when I stay at the hub, I am in touch with all the spokes at once.

To pray is to move to the center of all life and all love. The closer I come to the hub of life, the closer I come to all that receives its strength and energy from there. My tendency is to get so distracted by the diversity of the many spokes of life, that I am busy but not truly life-giving, all over the place but not focused. By directing my attention to the heart of life, I am connected with its rich variety while remaining centered. What does the hub represent? I think of it as my own heart, the heart of God, and the heart of the world. When I pray, I enter into the depth of my own heart and find there the heart of God, who speaks to me of love. And I recognize, right there, the place where all of my sisters and brothers are in communion with one another. The great paradox of the spiritual life is, indeed, that the most personal is most universal, that the most intimate, is most communal, and that the most contemplative is most active.

The wagon wheel shows that the hub is the center of all energy and movement, even when it often seems not to be moving at all. In God all action and all rest are one. So too prayer!

Chapter II

JOY

One: Joy and Sorrow

Joy is essential to spiritual life. Whatever we may think or say about God, when we are not joyful, our thoughts and words cannot bear fruit. Jesus reveals to us God's love so that his joy may become ours and that our joy may become complete. Joy is the experience of knowing that you are unconditionally loved and that nothing — sickness, failure, emotional distress, oppression, war, or even death — can take that love away.

Joy is not the same as happiness. We can be unhappy about many things, but joy can still be there because it comes from the knowledge of God's love for us. We are inclined to think that when we are sad we cannot be glad, but in the life of a God-centered person, sorrow and joy can exist together. That isn't easy to understand, but when we think about some of our deepest life experiences, such as being present at the birth of a child or the death of a friend, great sorrow and great joy are often seen to be parts of the same experience. Often we discover the joy in the midst of the sorrow. I remember the most painful times of my life as times in which I became aware of a spiritual reality much larger than myself, a reality that allowed me to live the pain with hope. I dare even to say: "My grief was the place where I found my joy." Still, nothing happens automatically in the spiritual life. Joy does not simply happen to us. We have to choose joy and keep choosing it every day. It is a choice based on the knowledge that we belong to God and have found in God our refuge and our safety and that nothing, not even death, can take God away from us.

Two: The Choice

It might sound strange to say that joy is the result of our choices. We often imagine that some people are luckier than others and that their joy or sorrow depends on the circumstances of their life — over which they have no control.

However, we do have a choice, not so much in regard to the circumstances of our life, but in regard to the way we respond to these circumstances. Two people can be the victims of the same accident. For the one, it becomes the source of resentment; for the other, the source of gratitude. The external circumstances are the same, but the choice of response is completely different. Some people become bitter as they grow old. Others grow old joyfully. That does not mean that the life of those who become bitter was harder than the life of those who become joyful. It means that different choices were made, inner choices, choices of the heart.

It is important to become aware that at every moment of our life we have an opportunity to choose joy. Life has many sides to it. There are always sorrowful and joyful sides to the reality we live. And so we always have a choice to live the moment as a cause for resentment or as a cause for joy. It is in the choice that our true freedom lies, and that freedom is, in the final analysis, the freedom to love.

It might be a good idea to ask ourselves how we develop our capacity to choose for joy. Maybe we could spend a moment at the end of each day and decide to remember that day — whatever may have happened — as a day to be grateful for. In so doing we increase our heart's capacity to choose for joy. And as our hearts become more joyful, we will become, without any special effort, a source of joy for others. Just as sadness begets sadness, so joy begets joy.

Three: Speaking about the Sun

Joy is contagious, just as sorrow is. I have a friend who radiates joy, not because his life is easy, but because he habitually recognizes God's presence in the midst of all human suffering, his own as well as others'. Wherever he goes, whomever he meets, he is able to see and hear something beautiful, something for which to be grateful. He doesn't deny the great sorrow that surrounds him nor is he blind or deaf to the agonizing sights and sounds of his fellow human beings, but his spirit gravitates toward the light in the darkness and the prayers in the midst of the cries of despair. His eyes are gentle; his voice is soft. There is nothing sentimental about him. He is a realist, but his deep faith allows him to know that hope is more real than despair, faith more real than distrust, and love more real than fear. It is this spiritual realism that makes him such a joyful man.

Whenever I meet him, I am tempted to draw his attention to the wars between nations, the starvation among children, the corruption in politics, and the deceit among people, thus trying to impress him with the ultimate brokenness of the human race. But every time I try something like this, he looks at me with his gentle and compassionate eyes and says: "I saw two children sharing their bread with one another, and I heard a woman say 'thank you' and smile when someone covered her with a blanket. These simple poor people gave me new courage to live my life."

My friend's joy is contagious. The more I am with him, the more I catch glimpses of the sun shining through the clouds. Yes, I know there is a sun, even though the skies are covered with clouds. While my friend always spoke about the sun, I kept speaking about the clouds, until one day I realized that it was the sun that allowed me to see the clouds.

Those who keep speaking about the sun while walking under a cloudy sky are messengers of hope, the true saints of our day.

Four: Surprised by Joy

Are we surprised by joy or by sorrow? The world in which we live wants to surprise us by sorrow. Newspapers keep telling us about traffic accidents, murders, conflicts between individuals, groups, and nations, and the television fills our minds with images of hatred, violence, and destruction. And we say to one another: "Did you hear that, did you see that... isn't it terrible... who can believe it?" Indeed it seems that the powers of darkness want to continue to surprise us with human sorrow. But these surprises paralyze us and seduce us to an existence in which our main concern becomes survival in the midst of a sea of sorrows. By making us think about ourselves as survivors of a shipwreck, anxiously clinging to a piece of driftwood, we gradually accept the role of victims doomed by the cruel circumstances of our lives.

The great challenge of faith is to be surprised by joy. I remember sitting at a dinner table with friends discussing the economic depression of the country. We kept throwing out statistics that made us increasingly convinced that things could only get worse.

Then, suddenly, the four-year-old son of one my friends opened the door, ran to his father, and said, "Look, Daddy! Look! I found a little kitten in the yard . . . Look! . . . Isn't she cute?" While showing the kitten to his father, the little boy stroked the kitten with his hands and held it against his face. All at once everything changed. The little boy and his kitten became the center of attention. There were smiles, strokes, and many tender words. We were surprised by joy!

God became a little child in the midst of a violent world. Are we surprised by joy or do we keep saying: "How nice and sweet, but the reality is different." What if the child reveals to us what is really real?

Five: Joy and Laughter

Money and success do not make us joyful. In fact many wealthy and successful people are also anxious, fearful, and often quite somber. In contrast, many others who are very poor laugh very easily and often show great joy.

Joy and laughter are the gifts of living in the presence of God and trusting that tomorrow is not worth worrying about. It always strikes me that rich people have much money, while poor people have much time. And when there is much time life can be celebrated. There is no reason to romanticize poverty, but when I see the fears and anxieties of many who have all the goods the world has to offer, I can understand Jesus' words: "How hard it is for the rich to enter the kingdom of God." Money and success are not the problem; the problem is the absence of free, open time when God can be encountered in the present and life can be lifted up in its simple beauty and goodness.

Little children playing together show us the joy of just being together. One day when I was very busy interviewing an artist whom I admire a lot, her five-year-old daughter said to me: "I made a birthday cake with sand. Now you have to come and pretend that you're eating it and that you like it. That will be fun!" The mother smiled and said to me: "You'd better play with her before you talk to me. Maybe she has more to teach you than I have."

The simple, direct joy of a small child reminds us that God seeks the places where there are smiles and laughter. Smiles and laughter open the doors to the kingdom. That's why Jesus calls us to be like children.

Six: No Victims

To be surprised by joy is something quite different from naive optimism. Optimism is the attitude that makes us believe that things will be better tomorrow. An optimist says: "The war will be over, your wounds will be healed, the depression will go away, the epidemic will be stopped.... All will be better soon." The optimist may be right or wrong, but, whether right or wrong, the optimist does not control the circumstances.

Joy does not come from positive predictions about the state of the world. It does not depend on the ups and downs of the circumstances of our lives. Joy is based on the spiritual knowledge that, while the world in which we live is shrouded in darkness, God has overcome the world. Jesus says it loudly and clearly: "In the world you will have troubles, but rejoice, I have overcome the world."

The surprise is not that, unexpectedly, things turn out better than expected. No, the real surprise is that

God's light is more real than all the darkness, that God's truth is more powerful than all human lies, that God's love is stronger than death.

The world lies in the power of the Evil One. Indeed, the powers of darkness rule the world. We should not be surprised when we see human suffering and pain all around us. But we should be surprised by joy every time we see that God, not the Evil One, has the last word. By entering into the world and confronting the Evil One with the fullness of Divine Goodness, the way was opened for us to live in the world, no longer as victims, but as free men and women, guided, not by optimism, but by hope.

Seven: The Fruit of Hope

There is an intimate relationship between joy and hope. While optimism makes us live as if someday soon things will go better for us, hope frees us from the need to predict the future and allows us to live in the present, with the deep trust that God will never leave us alone but will fulfill the deepest desires of our heart.

Joy in this perspective is the fruit of hope. When

I trust deeply that today God is truly with me and holds me safe in a divine embrace, guiding every one of my steps, I can let go of my anxious need to know how tomorrow will look, or what will happen next month or next year. I can be fully where I am and pay attention to the many signs of God's love within and around me.

We often speak about the "good old days," but when we think critically about them and let go of our romanticizing memories, we might soon discover that, during those very days, we were doing a lot of worrying about our future.

When we trust profoundly that today is the day of the Lord and that tomorrow is safely hidden in God's love, our faces can relax, and we can smile back at the One who smiles at us.

I remember once walking along the beach with a friend. We spoke intensely about our relationship, trying hard to explain ourselves to each other and to understand each other's feelings. We were so preoccupied with our mutual struggle that we didn't notice the magnificent sunset spreading a rich spectrum of color over the foam-capped waves breaking on the wide, silent beach.

Suddenly my friend exclaimed: "Look...look at the sun...look." He put his arm around my shoulder, and together we gazed at the shimmering ball of fire vanishing gradually below the horizon of the wide ocean.

At that moment, we both knew about hope and joy.

Eight: Beyond Wishes

Joy and hope are never separate. I have never met a hopeful person who was depressed or a joyful person who had lost hope. But hope is something other than wishes, and joy something other than happiness. Wishes and happiness generally refer to things or events. You wish that the weather will change or the war will end; you wish that you will get a new job, better pay, or a reward, and when you get what you wish, you are happy. But hope and joy are spiritual gifts rooted in an intimate relationship with the One who loves you with an everlasting love and who will always remain faithful to you. You hope in God and rejoice in God's presence even when your many wishes are not realized and you are not very happy with the circumstances of your life.

Some of the most hopeful and joyful moments of my life were moments of great emotional and physical pain. It was precisely during the experience of rejection or abandonment that I was "forced" to cry out to God: "You are my only hope, you are the source of my joy." When I could no longer cling to my normal supports I discovered that true support and real safety lie far beyond the structures of our world.

Often we have to come to the discovery that what we considered to be hope and joy were little more than quite selfish desires for success and rewards. Painful as this discovery may be, it can throw us right into the arms of the One who is the true source of all our hope and joy.

Chapter III

SUFFERING

One: Embracing the Pain

In the world about us, a radical distinction is made between joy and sorrow. People tend to say: "When you are glad, you cannot be sad, and when you are sad, you cannot be glad." In fact, our contemporary society does everything possible to keep sadness and gladness separated. Sorrow and pain must be kept away at all cost because they are the opposites of the gladness and happiness we desire.

Death, illness, human brokenness . . . all have to be hidden from our sight because they keep us from the happiness for which we strive. They are obstructions on our way to the goal of life.

The vision offered by Jesus stands in sharp contrast to this worldly vision. Jesus shows, both in his teachings and in his life, that true joy often is hidden in the midst of our sorrow, and that the dance of life finds its beginnings in grief. He says: "Unless the grain of wheat dies, it cannot bear fruit. . . . Unless we lose our lives, we cannot find them; unless the Son of Man dies, he cannot send the Spirit." To his two disciples who were dejected after his suffering and death, Jesus says: "You foolish people, so slow to believe all that the prophets have said! Was it not necessary that Christ should suffer and so enter into his glory?"

Here a completely new way of living is revealed. It is the way in which pain can be embraced, not out of a desire to suffer, but in the knowledge that something new will be born in the pain. Jesus calls our pains "labor pains." He says: "A woman in childbirth suffers because her time has come; but when she has given birth to the child, she forgets the suffering in her joy that a human being has been born into the world" (John 16:21)

The cross has become the most powerful symbol of this new vision. The cross is a symbol of death *and* of life, of suffering *and* of joy, of defeat *and* of victory. It's the cross that shows us the way.

Two: A Meal on a Tombstone

It will always remain very hard for us to embrace our suffering, trusting that it will lead to new life.

Nonetheless, there are experiences that demonstrate the truth of the way that Jesus shows. Let us look at just one.

A few years ago Bob, the husband of a friend of mine, died suddenly from a heart attack. My friend decided to keep her two young children away from the funeral. She thought: "It will be too hard for them to see their father put in the ground."

For years after Bob's death, the cemetery remained a fearful and dangerous place for them. Then, one day, my friend asked me to visit the grave with her and invited the children to come along. The elder was too afraid to go, but the younger decided to come with us. When we came to the place where Bob was buried, the three of us sat down on the grass around the stone engraved with the words: "A kind and gentle man." As we sat, we reminisced about Bob.

I said: "Maybe one day we should have a picnic here. . . . This is not only a place to think about death, but also a place to rejoice in our life. I think Bob will be most honored when we find new strength, here, to live." At first it seemed a strange idea: having a meal on top of a tombstone. But isn't that what Jesus told his disciples to do when he asked them to share bread and wine in his memory?

A few days later, my friend took her elder child to the grave. Her younger brother had convinced her that there was nothing to fear.

Now they often go to the cemetery and tell each other stories about Bob. No longer is Bob a stranger. He has become a new friend and having a picnic on his grave has become something to look forward to . . . at least when nobody is watching!

The tears of grief and the tears of joy shouldn't be too far apart. As we befriend our pain — or, in the words of Jesus, "take up our cross" — we discover that the resurrection is, indeed, close at hand.

Three: A Fellowship of the Weak

One very important way to befriend our sorrow is to take it out of its isolation, and share it with someone who can receive it. So much of our pain remains hidden — even from our closest friends. When we feel lonely, do we go to someone we trust and say: "I am lonely. I need your support and company." When we feel anxious, sexually needy, angry, or bitter, do we dare to ask a friend to be with us and receive our pain.

Too often we think or say: "I don't want to bother my friends with my problems. They have enough problems themselves." But the truth is that we honor our friends by entrusting our struggles to them. Don't we ourselves say to our friends who have hidden their feelings of fear and shame from us: "Why didn't you tell me, why did you keep it secret so long?" Obviously, not everyone can receive our hidden pains. But I believe that if we truly desire to grow in spiritual maturity, God will send us the friends we need.

So much of our suffering arises not just out of our painful condition, but from our feeling of isolation in the midst of our pain. Many people who suffer immensely from addiction — be it addiction to alcohol, drugs, sex, or food — find their first real relief when they can share their pain with others and discover that they are truly heard. The many twelve-step programs are a powerful witness to the truth that sharing our pain is the beginning of healing. Here we can see how close sorrow and joy can be. When I discover that I am no longer alone in my struggle and when I start experiencing a new "fellowship in weakness," then true joy can erupt, right in the middle of my sorrow.

But it is not easy to step out of our isolation. Somehow we always want to solve our problems on our own. But God has given us to each other to build a community of mutual love where we can discover together that joy is not just for others but for all of us.

Four: Beyond Individualism

Much of our isolation is self-chosen. We do not like to be dependent on others and, whenever possible, we try to show ourselves that we are in control of the situation and can make our own decisions. This self-reliance has many attractions. It gives us a sense of power, it allows us to move quickly, it offers us the satisfaction of being our own boss, and it promises many rewards and prizes.

However, the underside of this self-reliance is loneliness, isolation and a constant fear of not making it in life.

I have experienced the rewards as well as the punishments of individualism. As a university professor, I was a productive and popular teacher and made it through the many hoops of academic promotion, but at the very end of it all, I felt quite alone. Notwithstanding all the praise I was receiving while speaking about community, I didn't feel that I truly belonged to anyone. While showing convincingly the importance of prayer, I myself lost the ability to be quiet enough to pray. While encouraging mutual vulnerability as a way to grow in the Spirit, I found myself quite careful and even defensive where my own reputation was at stake. The bottom line for academics is competition — even for those who preach compassion — at least when they don't want to lose their jobs!

To make compassion the bottom line of life, to be open and vulnerable to others, to make community life the focus, and to let prayer be the breath of your life...that requires a willingness to tear down the countless walls that we have erected between ourselves and others in order to maintain our safe isolation. This is a lifelong and arduous spiritual battle because while tearing down walls with one hand, we build new ones with the other. After I had left the university and chosen a life in community, I realized that, even in community, there are numerous ways to play the controlling games of individualism. Indeed, true conversion asks for a lot more than a change of place. It asks for a change of heart.

Five: Our Desire for Communion

What do we really desire? As I try to listen to my own deepest yearning as well as to the yearnings of others, the word that seems best to summarize the desire of the human heart is "communion." Communion means "union with." God has given us a heart that will remain restless until it has found full communion. We look for it in friendship, in marriage, in community. We look for it in sexual intimacy, in moments of ecstasy, in the recognition of our gifts. We look for it through success, admiration, and rewards. But wherever we look, it is communion that we seek.

As I looked at the faces of the gold medalists at the Olympics, with more than sixty thousand people applauding them and millions watching them on television, I caught a glimpse of that momentary experience of communion. It seemed as if they had, finally, received the love they had worked for with unwavering dedication. And still, how soon they will be forgotten. Four, eight, or twelve years later, others will take their place on the platform of success, and their brief moment of glory will be remembered by very few.

Still, the desire for communion remains. It is a God-given desire, a desire that causes immense pain as well as immense joy. Jesus came to proclaim that our desire for communion is not in vain, but will be fulfilled by the One who gave us that desire. The passing moments of communion are only hints of the Communion that God has promised us. The real danger facing us is to distrust our desire for communion. It is a God-given desire without which our lives lose their vitality and our hearts grow cold. A truly spiritual life is life in which we won't rest until we have found rest in the embrace of the One who is the Father and Mother of all desires.

Six: Stepping over Our Wounds

We humans suffer a lot. Much, if not most, of our deep suffering comes from our relationships with those who love us. I am constantly aware that my deep agony and anguish come, not from the terrible events I read about in the newspapers or see on television, but from the relationships with the people with whom I share my daily life. The men and women who love me and are very close to me are also the ones who wound me. As we grow older, we often discover that we were not always loved well. Those who loved us often used us too. Those who cared for us were also envious at times. Those who gave us much, at times asked much in return. Those who protected us also wanted to possess us at critical moments. Often we feel the need to sort out how and why we are wounded and frequently we come to the frightening discovery that the love we received was not as pure and simple as we had thought.

It is important to sort these things out, especially when we feel paralyzed by fears, anxieties, and dark urges that we do not understand.

But understanding our wounds is not enough. Finally we must find the freedom to step over our wounds and the courage to forgive those who have wounded us. The real danger is to get stuck in anger and resentment. Then we start living as the "wounded one," always complaining that life isn't "fair."

Jesus came to save us from these self-destructive complaints. He says: "Let go of your complaints, forgive those who loved you poorly, step over your feelings of being rejected, and have the courage to trust that you won't fall into an abyss of nothingness but into the safe embrace of a God whose love will heal all your wounds."

Seven: Faithful to Our Vocation

On the television I see the emaciated faces of starving children in Somalia, and I want to help them. I read about the terrible plight of the Moslem people in Bosnia, desperately trying to survive under the unrelenting attacks of the Serbs, and I want to do something. Nelson Mandela is leading large rallies in South Africa to force the government to accept true democracy, and I would like to support him.

In Northern Ireland, Catholics and Protestants continue to kill each other, and I wonder how I should respond to that shameful situation. My priest friend, John Vesey, vicar of the diocese of Sololá in Guatemala, tells me that the genocide of Indians still continues, and I feel a deep desire to go there and offer him strength in his struggle against this unabating injustice. My friends in the Adam Morgan district in Washington, D.C., keep speaking to me about the increase of homelessness, drug traffic, killings, and general despair in their neighborhood, and I agonize about my responsibility in it all. In Toronto, close to where I live, more and more people, adults as well as small children, are dying of AIDS, and I ask myself constantly how to reach out to them.

The more I think about the human suffering in our world and my desire to offer a healing response, the more I realize how crucial it is not to allow myself to become paralyzed by feelings of impotence and guilt. More important than ever is to be very faithful to my vocation to do well the few things I am called to do and hold on to the joy and peace they bring me. I must resist the temptation to let the forces of darkness pull me into despair and make me one more of their many victims. I have to keep my eyes fixed on Jesus and on those who followed him and trust that I will know how to live out my mission to be a sign of hope in this world.

Eight: The Way of the Dalai Lama

I know of few people who have seen as much suffering as the Dalai Lama. As the spiritual and political leader of Tibet he was driven from his own country and witnessed the systematic killing, torture, oppression, and expulsion of his people.

Still, I know of few people who radiate so much peace and joy.

The Dalai Lama's generous and disarming laughter is free from any hatred or bitterness toward the Chinese who ravaged his land and murdered his people. He says: "They too are human beings who struggle to find happiness and deserve our compassion."

How is it possible that a man who has been subjected to such persecution is not filled with anger and a desire for revenge? When asked that question the Dalai Lama explains how, in his meditation, he allows all the suffering of his people and their oppressors to enter into the depth of his heart, and there to be transformed into compassion.

What a spiritual challenge! While I anxiously wonder how to help the people in Bosnia, South Africa, Guatemala and yes, Tibet ... the Dalai Lama calls me to gather all the suffering of the people of this world in the center of my being and to become there the raw material for my compassionate love.

Isn't that, too, the way of Jesus? Shortly before his death and resurrection, Jesus said: "When I am lifted up from the earth, I shall draw all people to myself." Jesus took upon himself the suffering of all people and made it into a gift of compassion to his Father. That, indeed, is the way for us to follow.

Nine: The Hurts of Love

Animals are frequently given to us to teach us love and compassion. In truth, I have very little interest in pets, be they dogs, cats, or parrots. Although I often get very irritated when pets become the main subject of conversation among friends, I must confess that one of the most vivid memories from my youth is connected with a little goat given to me by my father to care for during the last year of the Second World War. The goat's name was Walter. I was thirteen years old then, and we lived in a part of Holland that was isolated by the great rivers from the D-day armies. People were dying from hunger.

I loved my little goat. I spent hours collecting acorns for him, taking him on long walks, and playfully fighting with him, pushing him where his two horns were growing. I carried him in my arms, built a pen for him in the garage, and gave him a little wooden wagon to pull. As soon as I woke up in the morning, I fed him, and as soon as I returned from school I fed him again, cleaned his pen, and talked to him about all sorts of things. Indeed, my goat Walter and I were the best of friends.

One day, early in the morning when I entered the garage, I found the pen empty. Walter had been stolen. I don't remember ever having cried so vehemently and so long. I sobbed and screamed from grief. My father and mother hardly knew how to console me. It was the first time that I learned about love and loss.

Years later, when the war was over and we had enough food again, my father told me that our gardener had taken Walter and fed him to his family who had nothing left to eat. My father knew it was the gardener, but he never confronted him — even though he saw my grief. I now realize that both Walter and my father taught me something about compassion.

Chapter IV

CONVERSION

One: The Spirit of Love

While realizing that ten years ago I didn't have the faintest idea that I would end up where I now am, I still like to keep up the illusion that I am in control of my own life. I like to decide what I most need, what I will do next, what I want to accomplish, and how others will think of me. While being so busy running my own life, I become oblivious to the gentle movements of the Spirit of God within me, pointing me in directions quite different from my own.

It requires a lot of inner solitude and silence to become aware of these divine movements. God does not shout, scream, or push. The Spirit of God is soft and gentle like a small voice or a light breeze. It is the spirit of love. Maybe we still do not fully believe that God's Spirit is, indeed, the Spirit of love, always leading us deeper into love. Maybe we still distrust the Spirit, afraid to be led to places where our freedom is taken away. Maybe we still think of God's

Spirit as an enemy who wants something of us that is not good for us.

But God is love, only love, and God's Spirit is the Spirit of love longing to guide us to the place where the deepest desires of our heart can be fulfilled. Often we ourselves do not even know what our deepest desire is. We so easily get entangled in our own lust and anger, mistakenly assuming that they tell us what we really want.

The Spirit of love says: "Don't be afraid to let go of your need to control your own life. Let me fulfill the true desire of your heart."

Two: Turn Around

The words of Jesus, "Set your hearts on God's kingdom first...and all other things will be given you as well," summarize best the way we are called to live our lives. With our hearts set on God's kingdom. That kingdom is not some faraway land that we hope to reach, nor is it life after death or an ideal state of affairs. No. God's kingdom is, first of all, the active presence of God's spirit within us, offering us the freedom we truly desire.

And so the main question becomes: How to set our hearts on the kingdom first when our hearts are pre-occupied with so many things? Somehow a radical change of heart is required, a change that allows us to experience the reality of our existence from God's place.

Once I saw a mime in which a man was straining to open one of the three doors in the room where he found himself. He pushed and pulled at the door-knobs, but none of the doors would open. Then he kicked with his feet against the wooden panels of the door, but they didn't break. Finally, he threw his full weight against the doors, but none of them yielded.

It was a ridiculous, yet very hilarious sight, because the man was so concentrated on the three locked doors that he didn't even notice that the room had no back wall and that he could simply walk out if he would only turn around and look!

That is what conversion is all about. It is a complete turnaround that allows us to discover that we are not the prisoners we think we are. From God's place, we often look like one who tries to open the locked doors of a room. We worry about many things and even wound ourselves while worrying. God says:

"Turn around, set your heart on my kingdom. I give you all the freedom you desire."

Three: Answer from Above

It is remarkable that Jesus seldom answers the questions people bring to him. When the mother of James and John asked him to give her sons a place on his right or left side in the kingdom, he says: "Can you drink the cup that I am going to drink?" (Matthew 20:22). When the Sadducees tell Jesus about a woman who had seven husbands and then ask him whose wife she will be at the resurrection, he says: "At the resurrection men and women do not marry: no, they are like the angels in heaven" (Matthew 22:30). When the apostles asked him: "Lord, has the time come for you to restore the kingdom of Israel?" Jesus answers: "It is not for you to know times and dates that the Father has decided by his own authority, but you will receive the power of the Holy Spirit ...and you will be my witnesses" (Acts 1:7–8).

What is happening here? Jesus answers from above to questions raised from below. The mother of James and John is concerned about power and influence.

The Sadducees want Jesus to solve a theological problem, and the apostles want Jesus to liberate them from the Roman occupiers. But all their concerns come from below. They come from the complications caused by the powers of the world. Jesus does not answer from below. He answers from a place far beyond the powers of the world. His answers come from his most intimate communion with God.

For us to truly hear Jesus' answers, we need to be reborn from above. To Nicodemus he says: "In all truth I tell you, no one can see the kingdom of God without being reborn from above" (John 3:3).

The spiritual life is the life of those who are reborn from above — who have received the Spirit of God who comes to us from God. That life allows us to break out of our prison of human entanglements and sets us free for a life in God. Jesus says it clearly: "What is born of human nature is human, what is born of the Spirit is spirit" (John 3:6).

Four: Invitation to Conversion

In our ongoing search for meaning, we need to keep reading books and newspapers in a spiritual way. The question that should always be with us is: "Why are we living?" All the events of our short lives need to be interpreted. Books and newspapers are there to help us to read the signs of our times and so give meaning to our lives. Jesus says: "When you see a cloud looming up in the west you say at once that rain is coming, and so it does. And when the wind is from the south you say it's going to be hot, and it is. Hypocrites! You know how to interpret the face of the earth and the sky. How is it you do not know how to interpret these times?" (Luke 12:54–56).

Here lies the real challenge. Jesus does not look at the events of our times as a series of incidents and accidents that have little to do with us. Jesus sees the political, economic, and social events of our life as signs that call for a spiritual interpretation. They need to be read spiritually! But how?

Jesus himself shows us how. Once people had told Jesus the news that the governor Pilate had executed some rebellious men from Galilee and mingled their blood with that of the Roman sacrifices. When he heard this he said: "Do you suppose that these Galileans were worse sinners than any others, that this should happen to them? They were not. I tell you. No, but unless you repent you will all perish as they did" (Luke 13:2–3).

Jesus does not give a political interpretation of the event but a spiritual one: "What happened invites you to conversion!" This is the deepest meaning of history: a constant invitation calling us to turn our hearts to God and so discover the full meaning of our lives.

Five: Why AIDS?

Once we start reading the events of our time as calls to conversion, our perception of history changes radically. Ever since some friends of mine died of AIDS and ever since I have come to know the vast network of AIDS patients and those who work with and for them, I have been wondering about the "why" of it all. Why is this AIDS epidemic causing the death of thousands of people, young and old, men and women?

When John, the homosexual son of a dear friend in San Francisco, was struck with AIDS, the disease was no longer a faraway reality for me. I visited John during his illness. He introduced me to his gay friends and made me acutely aware of the immense physical and emotional suffering of countless young adults.

Jesus asks me: "Do you think that these men are worse sinners than you, that this should happen to them?" And I realize with a shock that the only possible answer is the answer: "No, they are not — but unless you repent, you will perish as they did." That answer turns everything upside down. The deaths of gay people call me to conversion!

What AIDS has shown is the dramatic connection between love and death. Gay men desperately looking for someone to love them found themselves being devoured by the powers of destruction and death. But God is the God of the living, not of the dead! God's love brings life, not death. My gay brothers are dying so that I may turn more radically to God and find there fulfillment for the yearnings of my body, mind, and heart. I must learn to read AIDS as one of the signs of our time, calling me to conversion. I pray for the courage to do so.

Six: The Reverse Mission

While living for a few months in one of the "young towns" surrounding Lima, Peru, I first heard the term, "reverse mission." I had come from the North to the South to help the poor, but the longer I was among the poor the more I became aware that there was another mission, the mission from the South to the North. When I returned to the North, I was deeply convinced that my main task would be to help the poor of Latin America convert their wealthy brothers and sisters in the United States and Canada.

Ever since that time, I have become aware that wherever God's Spirit is present there is a reverse mission.

When I marched with thousands of black and white Americans from Selma to Montgomery in the summer of 1965 to support the blacks in their struggle for equal rights, Martin Luther King already said that the deeper spiritual meaning of the civil rights movement was that the blacks were calling the whites to conversion.

When, years later, I joined L'Arche to live and work with mentally handicapped people, I soon learned that my real task would be to let those whom I wanted to help offer me — and through me many others — their unique spiritual gifts.

This "reversal" is the sign of God's Spirit. The poor

have a mission to the rich, the blacks have a mission to the whites, the handicapped have a mission to the "normal," the gay people have a mission to the straight, the dying have a mission to the living. Those whom the world has made into victims God has chosen to be bearers of good news.

When Jesus heard that eighteen people had been killed when the tower at Siloam had fallen down, he was asked whether these men and women were worse sinners than others. "They were not. I tell you," he said. "No, but unless you repent you will perish as they did." Jesus shows that the victims become our evangelists, calling us to conversion. That's the reverse mission that keeps surprising us.

Seven: God's Questions

Were the Jews who were killed in the gas chambers of the Nazi concentration camps more guilty than we are? What about the Maya Indians in Guatemala who were kidnapped, tortured, and executed by the military and the millions of Africans who starved to death...? And what about those who did the killing?

These are the questions from below, the questions we raise when we want to figure out who is better or worse than we are. But these are not questions from above. These are not God's questions. God does not ask us to define our little niche in humanity over and against other people. God's question is: "Are you reading the signs of your time as signs asking you to repent and be converted?" What really counts is our willingness to let the immense sufferings of our brothers and sisters free us from all arrogance and from all judgments and condemnations and give us a heart as gentle and humble as the heart of Jesus.

We spend countless hours making up our minds about others. An unceasing exchange of opinions about people close by or far away keeps us distracted and allows us to ignore the truth that we ourselves are the first ones who need a change of heart and probably the only ones whose hearts we indeed can change.

We always say again: "What about him? What about her?" What Jesus says to us, as he said to Peter, who wanted to know what would happen to John: "What does it matter to you. You are to follow me" (John 21:21–22).

Eight: The Burden of Judgment

Imagine having no need at all to judge anybody. Imagine having no desire to decide whether someone is a good or bad person. Imagine being completely free from the feeling that you have to make up your mind about the morality of someone's behavior. Imagine that you could say: "I am judging no one!"

Imagine — Wouldn't that be true inner freedom? The desert fathers from the fourth century said: "Judging others is a heavy burden." I have had a few moments in my life during which I felt free from all judgments about others. It felt as if a heavy burden had been taken away from me. At those moments I experienced an immense love for everyone I met, heard about, or read about. A deep solidarity with all people and a deep desire to love them broke down all my inner walls and made my heart as wide as the universe.

One such moment occurred after a seven-month stay in a Trappist monastery. I was so full of God's goodness that I saw that goodness wherever I went, even behind the façades of violence, destruction, and crime. I had to restrain myself from embracing the women and men who sold me groceries, flowers, and a new suit. They all seemed like saints to me!

We all have these moments if we are attentive to the movement of God's Spirit within us. They are like glimpses of heaven, glimpses of beauty and peace. It is easy to dismiss these moments as products of our dreams or poetic imagination. But when we choose to claim them as God's way of tapping us on our shoulders and showing us the deepest truth of our existence, we can gradually step beyond our need to judge others and our inclination to evaluate everybody and everything. Then we can grow toward real inner freedom and real sanctity.

But — we can only let go of the heavy burden of judging others when we don't mind carrying the light burden of being judged!

Nine: Claiming God's Love

Can we free ourselves from the need to judge others? Yes . . . by claiming for ourselves the truth that we are the beloved daughters and sons of God. As long as we continue to live as if we are what we do, what we have, and what other people think about us, we

70

will remain filled with judgments, opinions, evaluations, and condemnations. We will remain addicted to the need to put people and things in their "right" place. To the degree that we embrace the truth that our identity is not rooted in our success, power, or popularity, but in God's infinite love, to that degree can we let go of our need to judge.

"Do not judge, and you will not be judged; because the judgments you give are the judgments you will get" (Matthew 7:1). From this and all the other texts of the Gospel, it becomes clear that God's judgment is not the result of some divine calculation of which we have no part, but the direct reflection of our lack of trust in God's love. If we think of ourselves as the sum total of our successes, popularity, and power we become dependent on the ways we judge and are being judged and end up as victims manipulated by the world. And so we bring judgment on ourselves. Our death will mean not only the end of the exchange of judgments but also the end of ourselves, since we become nothing but the result of what we thought of others and what others thought of us.

Only when we claim the love of God, the love that transcends all judgments, can we overcome all fear of judgment. When we have become completely free from the need to judge others, we will also become completely free from the fear of being judged.

The experience of not having to judge cannot coexist with the fear of being judged, and the experience of God's non-judgmental love cannot coexist with a need to judge others. That's what Jesus means when he says: "Do not judge, and you will not be judged." The connection between the two sides of this sentence is the same connection that exists between the love of God and the love of neighbor. They cannot be separated. This connection, however, is not simply a logical connection that can be thought through. It is first and foremost a connection of the heart that is made in prayer.

Chapter V

DISCIPLINED LIVING

One: Living for the Gold

Reading the conclusion of chapter nine of Paul's first letter to the Corinthians, I can easily imagine that he has just been watching the Olympic games. He writes: "Do you not realize that, though all the runners in the stadium take part in the race, only one of them gets the prize? Run like that — to win. Every athlete concentrates completely on training, and this to win a wreath that will wither, whereas ours will never wither. So that is how I run, not without a clear goal; and how I box, not wasting blows on air. I punish my body and bring it under control, to avoid any risk that, having acted as herald for others, I myself may be disqualified."

More than two thousands years later, these words seem even more to the point than when they were first written. Watching on television the Barcelona '92 Olympics, I was deeply impressed, even somewhat overwhelmed, by the single-minded dedication and the vigorous discipline with which the athletes trained themselves to win the gold medal. Hundreds of runners, jumpers, divers, gymnasts, and other athletes had dedicated every part of their life to make it to that little platform of ultimate success.

I watched with special attention the Frenchman, Gatier, and the Swede, Waldner, in their final table-tennis match. The question that created nearly unbearable tension between the players and the thousands of onlookers, including King Gustav of Sweden and his wife, was: "Who of these two men will get the gold, and who will have to settle for the silver?"

With incredible virtuosity, the two rivals danced around the table returning the little yellow ball from far away and close by, outsmarting each other and constantly surprising their screaming fans. The power, speed, agility, and accuracy with which Waldner and Gatier made their points kept everyone guessing to the last second who would be the winner.

When, finally, the Swede was able to break the third tie and win the game 25/23, his tense and sober face exploded in a huge smile as he threw himself into the arms of his coach. It was the first gold medal for Sweden in the Barcelona Olympics. The thundering ovation in the sports hall and the enthusiasm of the Swedes suggested that something of ultimate importance had taken place.

When Paul saw a game like this, he wondered when we would have as much dedication and discipline to win the eternal glory as the athletes had to gain their wealth or medal. Maybe it would be helpful to think of the choir of saints, angels, and archangels as the enthusiastic onlookers and to realize that the King himself is watching us and hopes that he can give us the gold of his eternal love.

Two: A Clear Goal

Do we have a clear goal in life? The athletes whose clear goal is the attainment of the Olympic gold are willing to let everything else become secondary. The way they eat, sleep, study, and train are all determined by that one clear goal.

This is as true in the spiritual life as it is in the life of competitive sports. Without a clear goal, we will always be distracted and spend our energy on secondary things. "Keep your eye on the prize," Martin Luther King said to his people. What is our prize? Is it the divine life, the eternal life, the life with and in God. Jesus proclaimed to us that goal, that heavenly prize. To Nicodemus he said: "...this is how God loved the world: he gave his Son so that everyone who believes in him may not perish but may have eternal life" (John 3:16).

It is not easy to keep our eyes fixed on the eternal life, especially not in a world that keeps telling us that there are more immediate and urgent things on which to focus. There is scarcely a day that does not pull our attention away from our goal and make it look vague and cloudy. But still, we know from experience that without a clear goal our lives become fragmented into many tasks and obligations that drain us and leave us with a feeling of exhaustion and uselessness. How then do we keep our goal clear, how then do we fix our eyes on the prize? By the discipline of prayer: the discipline that helps us to bring God back again and again to the center of our life. We will always remain distracted, constantly busy with many urgent demands, but when there is a time and place set apart to return to our God who offers us eternal life, we gradually can come to realize that the many things we have to do, to say, or to think no longer distract us but are, instead, all leading us closer to our goal. Important, however, is that our goal remains clear. Prayer keeps our goal clear, and when our goal has become vague, prayer makes it clear again.

Three: Eternal Life

Eternal life. Where is it? When is it? For a long time I have thought about eternal life as a life after all my birthdays have run out. For most of my years I have spoken about the eternal life as the "afterlife," as "life after death." But the older I become, the less interest my "afterlife" holds for me. Worrying not only about tomorrow, next year, and the next decade, but even about the next life seems a false preoccupation. Wondering how things will be for me after I die seems, for the most part, a distraction. When my clear goal is the eternal life, that life must be reachable right now, where I am, because eternal life is life in and with God, and God is where I am here and now.

The great mystery of the spiritual life — the life in God — is that we don't have to wait for it as something that will happen later. Jesus says: "Dwell in me as I dwell in you." It is this divine in-dwelling that is eternal life. It is the active presence of God at the center of my living — the movement of God's Spirit within us — that gives us the eternal life.

But still, what about life after death? When we live in communion with God, when we belong to God's own household, there is no longer any "before" or "after." Death is no longer the dividing line. Death has lost its power over those who belong to God, because God is the God of the living, not of the dead. Once we have tasted the joy and peace that come from being embraced by God's love, we know that all is well and will be well. "Don't be afraid," Jesus says. "I have overcome the powers of death . . . come and dwell with me and know that where I am your God is."

When eternal life is our clear goal it is not a distant goal. It is a goal that can be reached in the present moment. When our heart understands this divine truth, we are living the spiritual life.

Four: *Spiritual Reading*

An important discipline in the life of the Spirit is spiritual reading. Through spiritual reading we have some say over what enters into our minds. Each day our society bombards us with a myriad of images and sounds. Driving down Yonge Street in downtown Toronto is like driving through a dictionary: each word demanding our attention in all sorts of sizes and colors and with all sorts of gestures and noises. The words yell and scream at us: "Eat me, drink me, buy me, hire me, look at me, talk with me, sleep with me"! Whether we ask for it or not is not the question; we simply cannot go far without being engulfed by words and images forcibly intruding themselves into our minds.

But do we really want our mind to become the garbage can of the world? Do we want our mind to be filled with things that confuse us, excite us, depress us, arouse us, repulse us, or attract us whether we think it is good for us or not? Do we want to let others decide what enters into our mind and determines our thoughts and feelings?

Clearly we do not, but it requires real discipline

to let God and not the world be the Lord of our mind. But that asks of us not just to be gentle as doves, but also cunning as serpents! Therefore spiritual reading is such a helpful discipline. Is there a book we are presently reading, a book that we have selected because it nurtures our mind and brings us closer to God? Our thoughts and feelings would be deeply affected if we were always to carry with us a book that puts our minds again and again in the direction we want to go. There are so many good books about the lives of holy men and women, about remarkable examples of peace-making, about communities that bring life to the poor and the oppressed, and about the spiritual life itself. Even if we were to read for only fifteen minutes a day in such a book, we would soon find our mind becoming less of a garbage can and more of a vase filled with good thoughts.

Five: Reading Spiritually

Spiritual reading is not only reading about spiritual people or spiritual things. It is also reading spiritually, that is, in a spiritual way! Reading in a spiritual way is reading with a desire to let God come closer to us.

Most of us read to acquire knowledge or to satisfy our curiosity. When we want to know how to repair a car, cook a meal, build a house, help a handicapped person, give a lecture, etc., we have to do a certain amount of reading. When we want to keep informed about world news, sports news, entertainment news, and society news, we must turn to different newspapers and magazines. The purpose of spiritual reading, however, is not to master knowledge or information, but to let God's Spirit master us. Strange as it may sound, spiritual reading means to let ourselves be read by God! We can read the story of Jesus' birth with curiosity and ask ourselves, "Did this really happen? Who put this story together and how?" But we can also read that same story with spiritual attentiveness and wonder: "How does God speak to me here and call me to a more generous love?" We can read the daily news simply to have something to talk about at work. But we can also read it to become more aware of the reality of a world that needs God's words and saving actions.

The issue is not just *what* we read, but *how* we

read it. Spiritual reading is reading with an inner attentiveness to the movement of God's Spirit in our outer and inner lives. With that attentiveness, we will allow God to read us and to explain to us what we are truly about.

Six: *In Search of Meaning*

The great value of spiritual reading is that it helps us to give meaning to our lives. Without meaning, human life quickly degenerates. The human person not only wants to live, but also wants to know why to live. Viktor Frankl, the psychiatrist, who wrote about his experiences in a German concentration camp during the Second World War, shows convincingly that without meaning in our lives we can't survive long. It is possible to live through many hardships when we believe that there still is someone or something worth living for. Food, drink, shelter, rest, friendship, and many other things are essential for life. But meaning is too!

It is remarkable how much of our life is lived without reflection on its meaning. It is not surprising that so many people are busy but bored! They have many things to do and are always running to get them done, but beneath the hectic activity they often wonder if anything is truly happening. A life that is not reflected upon eventually loses its meaning and becomes boring.

Spiritual reading is a discipline to keep us reflecting on our lives as we live them. When a child is born, friends get married, a parent dies, people revolt, or a nation starves, it's not enough just to know about these things and to celebrate, grieve, or respond as best we can. We have to keep asking ourselves: "What does it all mean? What is God trying to tell us? How are we called to live in the midst of all this?" Without such questions our lives become numb and flat.

But are there any answers? There are, but we will never find them unless we are willing to live the questions first and trust that, as Rilke says, we will, without even noticing it, grow into the answer. When we keep the Bible and our spiritual books in one hand and the newspaper in the other, we will always discover new questions, but we also will discover a way to live them faithfully, trusting that gradually the answer will be revealed to us.

Chapter VI

THE SPIRITUAL LIFE

One: The Still Small Voice

I am constantly puzzled by my eagerness to get something done, to see someone, to finish some job, while I am fully aware that within a month or even a week I will have completely forgotten what it was that seemed so urgent. It seems that I share this restlessness with many others.

Recently I was standing at the corner of Bloor and Yonge streets in downtown Toronto. I saw a young man crossing the street while the stoplight turned red. He just missed being hit by a car. Meanwhile, hundreds of people were moving in all directions. Most faces looked quite tense and serious, and no one greeted anyone. They were all absorbed in their own thoughts, trying to reach some unknown goal. Long rows of cars and trucks were crossing the intersection or making right and left turns in the midst of the large pedestrian crowd.

I wondered: "What is going on in the minds of

all these people. What are they trying to do, what are they hoping for, what is pushing them?" As I stood at that busy intersection, I wished I were able to overhear the inner ruminations of all these people. But I soon realized that I didn't have to be so curious. My own restlessness was probably not very different from that of all those around me!

Why is it so difficult to be still and quiet and let God speak to me about the meaning of my life. Is it because I don't trust God? Is it because I don't know God? Is it because I wonder if God really is there for me? Is it because I am afraid of God? Is it because everything else is more real for me than God? Is it because, deep down, I do not believe that God cares what happens at the corner of Yonge and Bloor?

Still there is a voice — right there, in downtown Toronto. "Come to me, you who labor and are over burdened, and I will give you rest. Shoulder my yoke and learn from me, for I am gentle and humble in heart, and you will find rest for your soul. Yes, my yoke is easy and my burden light" (Matthew 11:28–30).

Can I trust that voice and follow it? It is not a very loud voice, and often it is drowned out by the clamor of the inner city. Still, when I listen attentively, I will hear that voice again and again and come to recognize it as the voice speaking to the deepest places of my heart.

Two: Do You Love Me?

The simple statement, "God is love," has far-reaching implications the minute we begin living our lives based on that statement. When God who has created me is love and only love, I am loved before any human being loved me.

When I was a small child I kept asking my father and mother: "Do you love me?" I asked that question so often and so persistently that it became a source of irritation to my parents. Even though they assured me hundreds of times that they loved me I never seemed fully satisfied with their answers and kept on asking the same question. Now, many years later, I realize that I wanted a response they couldn't give. I wanted them to love me with an everlasting love. I know that this was the case because my question, "Do you love me?" was always accompanied by the question, "Do I have to die?"

Somehow, I must have known that if my parents would love me with a total, unlimited, unconditional love, I would never die. And so I kept pestering the parents with the strange hope that I would be an exception to the general rule that all people are going to die one day.

Much of our energy goes into the question: "Do you love me?" As we grow older, we develop many more subtle and sophisticated ways of asking that question. We say: "Do you trust me, do you care for me, do you appreciate me, are you faithful to me, will you support me, will you speak well of me, and so on and on." Much of our pain comes from our experience of not having been loved well.

The great spiritual challenge is to discover, over time, that the limited, conditional, and temporal love we receive from parents, husbands, wives, children, teachers, colleagues and friends are reflections of the unlimited, unconditional, and everlasting love of God. Whenever we can make that huge leap of faith we will know that death is no longer the end but the gateway to the fullness of the Divine Love.

Three: From Fatalism to Faith

We are always tempted with fatalism. When we say, "Well I have always been impatient; I guess I have to live with it," we are being fatalistic. When we say, "That man never had a loving father or mother; you shouldn't be surprised that he ended up in prison," we speak as fatalists. When we say, "She was terribly abused as a child; how do you expect her to ever have a healthy relationship with a man," we allow fatalism to overshadow us. When we say, "The wars between nations, the starvation of millions of people, the AIDS epidemics, and the economic depression all over the world all prove that there is little reason for hope," we have become victims of fatalism.

Fatalism is the attitude that makes us live as passive victims of exterior circumstances beyond our control.

The opposite of fatalism is faith. Faith is the deep trust that God's love is stronger than all the anonymous powers of the world and can transform us from victims of darkness into servants of light.

After Jesus drove out the demon from a lunatic boy, his disciples asked him: "Why were we unable to cast it out?" Jesus answered: "Because you have little faith. I tell you solemnly, if your faith were the size of a mustard seed, you could say to this mountain, move from here to there and it would move; nothing would be impossible for you" (Matthew 17:19–20).

It is important to identify the many ways in which we think, speak, or act with fatalism and, step by step, to convert them into moments of faith. This movement from fatalism to faith is the movement that will remove the cold darkness from our hearts and transform us into people whose trust in the power of love can, indeed, make mountains move.

Four: Under the Cross

It is so hard to keep looking at life from above, from God's place. Recently my dear friend Jonas called me. With a broken voice he told me that his daughter, Rebecca, had died four hours after her birth. Jonas, his wife, Margaret, and their little son, Samuel, had been so much looking forward to the new baby. She was born prematurely but still able to live. However, it soon became clear that she would not live long.

Jonas baptized little Rebecca; he and Margaret held her for a while and then it was all over.

Jonas said: "As I drove away from the hospital, I kept saying to God: 'Dear God, you gave Rebecca to me; now I give her back to you.' But it is such a pain, such a cutting away of a beautiful future, such a feeling of emptiness."

"Rebecca is your daughter," I said, "and she always will remain your and Margaret's daughter. She has been given to you for only a few hours, but those few hours are not in vain. Trust that Samuel has a sister and that Margaret, and you have a daughter dwelling in God's eternal embrace. You signed her with the sign of the cross of Jesus with which Samuel, Margaret and you have been signed, and under that sign your love will grow deeper and wider even when your heart is pierced."

We spoke a long time on the phone. We so much wanted to hold each other and cry together; we so much wanted to just be together and find some consolation in each other's friendship.

Why is this happening? So that God's glory can be revealed? It is so hard to say "Yes" to that when all is dark.

I look at Mary holding the dead body of Jesus on her lap. I think of Margaret and Jonas holding little Rebecca in their arms. And I pray.

Five: The Grateful Life

How can we live a truly grateful life? When we look back at all that has happened to us, we easily divide our lives into good things to be grateful for and bad things to forget. But with a past thus divided, we cannot move freely into the future. With many things to forget we can only limp toward the future.

True spiritual gratitude embraces all of our past, the good as well as the bad events, the joyful as well as the sorrowful moments. From the place where we stand, everything that took place brought us to this place, and we want to remember all of it as part of God's guidance. That does not mean that all that happened in the past was good, but it does mean that even the bad didn't happen outside the loving presence of God.

Jesus' own suffering was brought upon him by the forces of darkness. Still he speaks about his suffering and death as his way to glory.

It is very hard to keep bringing all of our past under the light of gratitude. There are so many things about which we feel guilt and shame, so many things we simply wish had never happened. But each time we have the courage to look at "the all of it" and to look at it as God looks at it, our guilt becomes a happy guilt and our shame a happy shame because they have brought us to a deeper recognition of God's mercy, a stronger conviction of God's guidance, and a more radical commitment to a life in God's service.

Once all of our past is remembered in gratitude, we are free to be sent into the world to proclaim good news to others. Just as Peter's denials didn't paralyze him but, once forgiven, became a new source of his faithfulness, so can all our failures and betrayals be transformed into gratitude and enable us to become messengers of hope.

Six: The Blessings from the Poor

Jean Vanier, the Canadian who founded a worldwide network of communities for mentally disabled people, has remarked more than once that Jesus did not say: "Blessed are those who care for the poor," but

"Blessed are the poor." Simple as this remark may seem, it offers the key to the kingdom.

I want to help. I want to do something for people in need. I want to offer consolation to those who are in grief and alleviate the suffering of those who are in pain. There is obviously nothing wrong with that desire. It is a noble and grace-filled desire. But unless I realize that God's blessing is coming to me from those I want to serve, my help will be short-lived, and soon I will be "burned out."

How is it possible to keep caring for the poor when the poor only get poorer? How is it possible to keep nursing the sick when they are not getting better? How can I keep consoling the dying when their deaths only bring me more grief? The answer is that they all hold a blessing for me, a blessing that I need to receive. Ministry is, first of all, receiving God's blessing from those to whom we minister. What is this blessing? It is a glimpse of the face of God. Seeing God is what heaven is all about! We can see God in the face of Jesus, and we can see the face of Jesus in all those who need our care.

Once I asked Jean Vanier: "How do you find the strength to see so many people each day and listen to their many problems and pains?" He gently smiled and said: "They show me Jesus and give me life." Here lies the great mystery of Christian service. Those who serve Jesus in the poor will be fed by him whom they serve: "He will put on an apron, set them down at table and wait on them" (Luke 12:37).

We so much need a blessing. The poor are waiting to bless us.

Seven: Adam's Gift

Only gradually are we discovering the blessings that the poor have to offer to those who care for them. This became clear to me when, one day, Father Bruno, the former abbot of a contemplative monastery, came to the L'Arche Daybreak community to spend a few months with us. The community asked him to live in one of the homes called the "New House" and care for Adam.

Adam is a deeply handicapped man. Adam cannot speak nor walk by himself. Adam cannot recognize individual people, nor is he able to communicate with signs. He needs constant help in everything. Getting up, taking a bath, getting dressed, brushing his teeth, shaving, and combing his hair. The only thing he can do by himself is eat! He loves to eat, and with a spoon, held firmly in his hand, he can bring his food from his plate to his mouth. He also can hold a glass or cup and drink his milk or juice by himself.

Bruno came to love Adam. He gave him all his time and attention. For three months Bruno and Adam were very close companions.

When Bruno left, he came to see me and said: "As abbot I have given many talks about the spiritual life and tried to live it myself. I have studied *The Cloud of Unknowing* and other mystical writings; I always knew that I had to become empty for God, gradually letting go of thoughts, emotions, feelings, and passions that prevented that deep communion I desired. When I met Adam, I met a man who, while considered by the world as profoundly disabled, was chosen by God to be bearer of a profound grace of God's presence. As I spent many hours and many days with Adam, I found myself drawn to a deep inner quiet. In Adam's 'emptiness' there was present to me — as there had been for others — a fullness of divine love, a powerful attraction to the mystical life; that is, the life in communion with God." Bruno's words touched me deeply and made me aware that God had sent Adam to Bruno to be his spiritual guide.

Eight: Two by Two

Traveling is seldom good for the spiritual life. Especially traveling alone. Airplanes, airports, busses and bus terminals, trains and railroad stations filled with people moving here and there, cluttered with magazines, books, and useless objects — it's all too much, too sensual and distracting to keep our hearts and minds focused on God. When I travel alone I eat too much, drink too much, and look around too much. Meanwhile, I let my mind wander to unhealthy, imaginary places and allow my heart to drift along with confusing emotions and feelings.

Jesus doesn't want us to travel alone. He sends us out two by two, saying: "Look, I am sending you out like sheep among wolves, so be cunning as snakes and yet innocent as doves."

Since I live in the Daybreak community, a community with people with mental disabilities, I seldom travel alone. The community sends me out with Bill,

Francis, David, Peter, and many other handicapped members, not just because they love to travel but also because I need their support. And what a difference that makes!

Traveling together radically shifted the significance of my trips. Instead of lecture trips they became missions, instead of situations full of temptations they became spiritual adventures, instead of times of loneliness they became opportunities for community.

The words of Jesus, "Where two or three are gathered in my name I am in their midst," have became very real for me. Together we are well protected against the seductive powers surrounding us and together we can reveal something of God that none of us is able to reveal on our own. Together, indeed, we can be as cunning as snakes and as innocent as doves.

Chapter VII

PRAYER

One: Mother Teresa's Answer

Once, quite a few years ago, I had the opportunity of meeting Mother Teresa of Calcutta. I was struggling with many things at the time and decided to use the occasion to ask Mother Teresa's advice. As soon as we sat down I started explaining all my problems and difficulties — trying to convince her of how complicated it all was! When, after ten minutes of elaborate explanation, I finally became silent, Mother Teresa looked at me quietly and said: "Well, when you spend one hour a day adoring your Lord and never do anything which you know is wrong...you will be fine!"

When she said this, I realized, suddenly, that she had punctured my big balloon of complex self-complaints and pointed me far beyond myself to the place of real healing. In fact, I was so stunned by her answer that I didn't feel any desire or need to continue the conversation. The many people waiting outside the room to see her could probably use her time better than I. So I thanked her and left.

Her few words became engraved on my heart and mind and remain to this day. I had not expected these words, but in their directness and simplicity, they cut through to the center of my being. I knew that she had *spoken* the truth and that I had the rest of my life to *live* it.

Reflecting on this brief but decisive encounter, I realize that I had raised a question from below and that she had given an answer from above. At first, her answer didn't seem to fit my question, but then I began to see that her answer came from God's place and not from the place of my complaints. Most of the time we respond to questions from below with answers from below. The result is more questions and more answers and, often, more confusion.

Mother Teresa's answer was like a flash of lightning in my darkness. I suddenly knew the truth about myself.

Two: From Worrying to Prayer

One of the least helpful ways to stop worrying is to try hard not to think about the things we are worrying about. We cannot push away our worries with our minds. When I lay in my bed worrying about an upcoming meeting, I can't stop my worries by saying to myself: "Don't think about these things; just fall asleep. Things will work out fine tomorrow." My mind simply answers: "How do you know?" and is back worrying again.

Jesus' advice to set our hearts on God's kingdom is somewhat paradoxical. You might give it the following interpretation: "If you want to worry, worry about that which is worth the effort. Worry about larger things than your family, your friends, or tomorrow's meeting. Worry about the things of God: truth, life, and light!"

As soon, however, as we set our hearts on these things our minds stop spinning because we enter into communion with the One who is present to us here and now and is there to give us what we most need. And so worrying becomes prayer, and our feelings of powerlessness are transformed into a consciousness of being empowered by God's spirit.

Indeed, we cannot prolong our lives by worrying, but we can move far beyond the boundaries of our short life span and claim eternal life as God's beloved children.

Does that put an end to our worrying? Probably not. As long as we are in our world, full of tensions and pressures, our minds will never be free from worries, but when we keep returning with our hearts and minds to God's embracing love, we will be able to keep smiling at our own worrisome selves and keep our eyes and ears open for the sights and sounds of the kingdom.

Three: From Mind to Heart

How do we concretely go about setting our hearts on God's kingdom? When I lay in my bed, not able to fall asleep because of my many worries, when I do my work preoccupied about all the things that can go wrong, when I can't get my mind off my concern for a dying friend — what am I supposed to do? Set my heart on the kingdom? Fine, but how does one do this?

There are as many answers to this question as there are people with different lifestyles, personalities, and external circumstances. There is not one specific answer that fits everyone's needs. But there are some answers that can offer helpful directions.

One simple answer is to move from the mind to the heart by slowly saying a prayer with as much attentiveness as possible. This may sound like offering a crutch to someone who asks you to heal his broken leg. The truth, however, is that a prayer, prayed from the heart, heals. When you know the Our Father, the Apostles' Creed, the "Glory Be to the Father" by heart, you have something to start with. You might like to learn by heart the Twenty-third Psalm: "The Lord is my shepherd . . . " or Paul's words about love to the Corinthians or St. Francis's prayer: "Lord, make me an instrument of your peace. . . . " As you lie in your bed, drive your car, wait for the bus, or walk your dog, you can slowly let the words of one of these prayers go through your mind simply trying to listen with your whole being to what they are saying. You will be constantly distracted by your worries, but if you keep going back to the words of the prayer, you will gradually discover that your worries become less obsessive and that you really start to enjoy praying. And as the prayer descends from your mind into the center of your being you will discover its healing power.

Four: Nothing Is Wanting!

Why is the attentive repetition of a well-known prayer so helpful in setting our hearts on the kingdom? It is helpful because the words of such a prayer have the power to transform our inner anxiety into inner peace.

For a long time, I prayed the words, "The Lord is my shepherd; there is nothing I shall want. Fresh and green are the pastures where he gives me repose. Near restful waters he leads me to revive my drooping spirit." I prayed these words in the morning for half an hour sitting quietly on my chair trying only to keep my mind focused on what I was saying. I prayed them during the many moments of the day when I was going here or there, and I even prayed them during my routine activities. The words stand in stark contrast to the reality of my life. I want many things; I see mostly busy roads and ugly shopping malls; and if there are any waters to walk along they are mostly polluted. But as I keep saying: "The Lord is my shepherd..." and allow God's shepherding love to enter more fully into my heart, I become more fully aware that the busy roads, the ugly malls, and the polluted waterways are not telling the true story of who I am. I do not belong to the powers and principalities that rule the world but to the Good Shepherd who knows his own and is known by his own. In the presence of my Lord and Shepherd there truly is nothing I shall want. He will, indeed, give me the rest my heart desires and pull me out of the dark pits of my depression.

It is good to know that millions of people have prayed these same words over the centuries and found comfort and consolation in them. I am not alone when I pray these words. I am surrounded by countless women and men, those who are close by and those who are far away, those who are presently living and those who have died recently or long ago, and I know that long after I have left this world these same words will continue to be prayed until the end of time.

The deeper these words enter into the center of my being, the more I become part of God's people and the better I understand what it means to be in the world without being of it.

Five: Contemplating the Gospel

Whatever concrete method we use to set our minds and hearts on the kingdom, it is important only in that it brings us closer to our Lord. The attentive repetition of a prayer is one method that has proven to be fruitful. Another is the contemplation of the daily Gospel. Each day of the year has its own Gospel passage. Each passage holds its own treasure for us. For me it has been of immense spiritual value to read each morning the story about Jesus that has been chosen for the day and to look at it and listen to it with my inner eyes and ears. I have discovered that when I do this over a long period of time, the life of Jesus becomes more and more alive in me and starts to guide me in my daily activities.

Often I have found myself saying: "The Gospel that I read this morning was just what I needed today!" This was much more than a wonderful coincidence. What, in fact, was taking place was not that a Gospel text helped me with a concrete problem, but that the many Gospel passages that I had been contemplating were gradually giving me new eyes and new ears to see and hear what was happening in the world. It wasn't that the Gospel proved useful for my many worries but that the Gospel proved the uselessness of my worries and so refocused my whole attention.

Once I was trying very hard to help two of my friends resolve their marriage difficulties. As I read the Gospel stories day after day it dawned on me that I was more interested in being a successful counselor than in making my friends fully open to God's will, whatever the implications would be for their future life. I became less anxious to solve their problems and more free to be an instrument of God's healing.

The daily contemplation of the Gospel is one of the most straightforward ways to set our minds and hearts first on the kingdom.

Six: Pictures on Our Inner Walls

The daily contemplation of the Gospel and the attentive repetition of a prayer can both profoundly affect our inner life. Our inner life is like a holy space that needs to be kept in good order and well decorated. Prayer, in whatever form, is the way to make our inner room a place where we can welcome those people who search for God.

After I had spent a few weeks slowly repeating Paul's words, "Love is always patient and kind; love is never jealous — love never seeks its own advantage," these words began to appear on the walls of my inner room much as the license in a doctor's office. This was obviously not an "apparition" but the emergence of an image. This image of a picture with sacred words on the wall of my inner room gave me a new understanding of the relationship between prayer and ministry.

Whenever I meet people during the day, I receive them in my inner room, trusting that the pictures on my walls will guide our meeting.

Over the years, many new pictures have appeared on my inner walls. Some show words, some gestures of blessing, forgiveness, reconciliation, and healing. Many show faces: the faces of Jesus and Mary, the faces of Thérèse of Lisieux and Charles de Foucauld, the faces of Ramakrishna and the Dalai Lama.

It is very important that our inner room has pictures on its walls, pictures that allow those who enter our lives to have something to look at that tells them where they are and where they are invited to go. Without prayer and contemplation the walls of our inner room will remain barren, and few will be inspired.

Seven: A Spiritual Milieu

We cannot live a spiritual life alone. The life of the Spirit is like a seed that needs fertile ground to grow. This fertile ground includes not only a good inner disposition, but also a supportive milieu.

It is very hard to live a life of prayer in a milieu where no one prays or speaks lovingly about prayer. It is nearly impossible to deepen our communion with God when those with whom we live and work reject or even ridicule the idea that there is a loving God. It is a superhuman task to keep setting our hearts on the kingdom when all those whom we know and talk with are setting their hearts on everything but the kingdom.

It is not surprising that people who live in a secular milieu — where God's name is never mentioned, prayer unknown, the Bible never read, and conversation about the life in the Spirit completely absent — cannot sustain their communion with God for very long. I have discovered how sensitive I am to the milieu in which I live. With my community, words about God's presence in our life come spontaneously and with great ease. However, when I join in a business meeting in downtown Toronto or keep company with those who work with AIDS patients, a conversation about God often creates embarrassment or even anger and generally ends up in a debate about the pros and cons of religion that leaves everybody unhappy.

When we are serious about living a spiritual life we are responsible for the milieu where it can grow and mature. Although we might not be able to create the ideal context for a life in the Spirit, we have many more options than we often claim for ourselves. We can choose friends, books, churches, art, music, places to visit, and people to be with that, taken together, offer a milieu that allows the mustard seed that God has sown in us to grow into a strong tree.

Chapter VIII

COMPASSION

One: From Competition to Compassion

If there is one notion that is central to all great religions it is that of "compassion." The sacred scriptures of the Hindus, Buddhists, Moslems, Jews, and Christians all speak about God as the God of compassion. In a world in which competition continues to be the dominant mode of relating among people, be it in politics, sports, or economics, all true believers proclaim compassion, not competition, as God's way.

How is it possible to make compassion the center of our lives? As insecure, anxious, vulnerable, and mortal beings — always involved, somehow and somewhere, in the struggle for survival — competition seems to offer us a great deal of satisfaction. In the Olympics, as well as in the American presidential race, it is clear that winning is what is most desired and most admired.

Still, Jesus says: "Be compassionate as your heavenly Father is compassionate," and throughout the centuries all great spiritual guides echo these words. Compassion — which means, literally, "to suffer with" — is the way to the truth that we are most ourselves, not when we differ from others, but when we are the same. Indeed, the main spiritual question is not, "What difference do you make?" but "What do you have in common?" It is not "excelling" but "serving" that makes us most human. It is not proving ourselves to be better than others but confessing to be just like others that is the way to healing and reconciliation.

Compassion, to be with others when and where they suffer and to willingly enter into a fellowship of the weak, is God's way to justice and peace among people. Is this possible? Yes, it is, but only when we dare to live with the radical faith that we do not have to compete for love, but that love is freely given to us by the One who calls us to compassion.

Two: Being the Beloved

Jesus shows us the way of compassion, not only by what he says, but also by how he lives. Jesus speaks and lives as the Beloved Son of God. One of the most central events of Jesus' life is related by Matthew: "When Jesus had been baptized he at once came up from the water, and suddenly, the heavens opened and he saw the Spirit of God descending like a dove and coming down on him. And suddenly there was a voice from heaven, 'This is my Son, the Beloved: my favor rests on him' " (Matthew 3:16–17).

This event reveals the true identity of Jesus. Jesus is the Beloved of God. This spiritual truth will guide all his thoughts, words, and actions. It is the rock on which his compassionate ministry will be built. This becomes very obvious when we are told that the same Spirit who descended on him when he came up from the water, also led him into the desert to be tempted. There the "Tempter" came to him asking him to prove that he was worth being loved. The "Tempter" said to him: "Do something useful, like turning stones into bread. Do something sensational, like throwing yourself down from a high tower. Do something that brings you power, like paying me homage." These three temptations were three ways to seduce Jesus into becoming a competitor for love. The world of the "Tempter" is precisely that world in which people compete for love through doing useful, sensational, and powerful things and so winning medals that gain them affection and admiration.

Jesus, however, is very clear in his response: "I don't have to prove that I am worthy of love. I am the Beloved of God, the One on whom God's favor rests." It was that victory over the "Tempter" that set Jesus free to choose for the compassionate life.

Three: Downward Mobility

The compassionate life is the life of downward mobility! In a society in which upward mobility is the norm, downward mobility is not only discouraged but even considered unwise, unhealthy, or downright stupid. Who will freely choose a low-paying job when a high-paying job is being offered? Who will choose poverty when wealth is within reach? Who will choose a hidden place when there is a place in the limelight? Who will choose to be with one person in great need when many people could be helped during the same time? Who will choose to withdraw to a place of solitude and prayer when there are so many urgent demands made from all sides?

My whole life I have been surrounded by well-meaning encouragement to go "higher up," and the most-used argument was: "You can do so much good there, for so many people."

But these voices calling me to upward mobility are completely absent from the Gospel. Jesus says: "Anyone who loves his life loses it; anyone who hates his life in this world will keep it for the eternal life" (John 12:25). He also says: "Unless you become like little children you will never enter the kingdom of heaven" (Matthew 18:3). Finally he says: "You know that among the gentiles the rulers lord it over them, and great men make their authority felt; among you this is not to happen. No; anyone who wants to become great among you must be your servant, and anyone who wants to be first among you must be your slave, just as the Son of Man came, not to be served, but to serve, and to give his life as a ransom for many" (Matthew 20:25–28).

This is the way of downward mobility, the descending way of Jesus. It is the way toward the poor, the suffering, the marginal, the prisoners, the refugees, the lonely, the hungry, the dying, the tortured, the homeless — toward all who ask for compassion.

What do they have to offer? Not success, popularity, or power, but the joy and peace of the children of God.

Four: The Secret Gift of Compassion

Downward mobility, moving toward those who suffer and sharing in their pain, seems close to being masochistic and even morbid. What joy can there be in solidarity with the poor, the sick, and the dying? What joy can there be in compassion?

People like Francis of Assisi, Charles de Foucauld, Mahatma Gandhi, Albert Schweizter, Dorothy Day, and many others were far from masochistic or morbid. They all radiated with joy. This, obviously, is a joy largely unknown to our world. When we go by what the media tell us, joy should come from success, popularity, and power, even though those who have these things are often quite heavy of heart and even depressed.

The joy that compassion brings is one of the best-kept secrets of humanity. It is a secret known to only a very few people, a secret that has to be rediscovered over and over again.

I have had a few glimpses of it. When I came to Daybreak, a community with people who have mental disabilities, I was asked to spend a few hours with Adam, one of the handicapped members of the community. Each morning I had to get him out of bed, give him a bath, shave him, brush his teeth, comb his hair, dress him, walk him to the kitchen, give him his breakfast, and bring him to the place where he spends his day. During the first few weeks, I was mostly afraid, always worrying that I would do something wrong or that he would have an epileptic seizure. But gradually I relaxed and started to enjoy our daily routine. As the weeks passed by, I discovered how I had come to look forward to my two hours with Adam. Whenever I thought of him during the day, I experienced gratitude for having him as my friend. Even though he couldn't speak or even give a sign of recognition, there was real love between us. My time with Adam had become the most precious time of the day. When a visiting friend asked me one day: "Couldn't you spend your time better than working with this handicapped man? Was it for this type of work that you got all your education?" I realized that I couldn't explain to him the joy that Adam brought me. He had to discover that for himself.

Joy is the secret gift of compassion. We keep forgetting it and thoughtlessly look elsewhere. But each time we return to where there is pain, we get a new glimpse of the joy that is not of this world.

Five: Right Where We Are

It would be sad if we were to think about the compassionate life as a life of heroic self-denial. Compassion, as a downward movement toward solidarity instead of an upward movement toward popularity, does not require heroic gestures or a sensational turnaround. In fact, the compassionate life is mostly hidden in the ordinariness of everyday living. Even the lives of those whom we look up to for their examples of compassion show that the descending way toward the poor was, first of all, practiced through small gestures in everyday life.

The question that truly counts is not whether we imitate Mother Teresa, but whether we are open to the many little sufferings of those with whom we share our life. Are we willing to spend time with those who do not stimulate our curiosity? Do we listen to those who do not immediately attract us? Can we be compassionate to those whose suffering remains hidden from the eyes of the world. There is much hidden suffering: the suffering of the teenager who does not feel secure; the suffering of the husband and wife who feel that there is no love left between them; the suffering of the wealthy executive who thinks that people are more interested in his money than in him; the suffering of the gay man or woman who feels isolated from family and friends; the suffering of the countless people who lack caring friends, satisfying work, a peaceful home, a safe neighborhood; the suffering of the millions who feel lonely and wonder if life is worth living.

Once we look downward instead of upward on the ladder of life, we see the pain of people wherever we go, and we hear the call of compassion wherever we are. True compassion always begins right where we are.

Six: Suffering with Others

Compassion is something other than pity. Pity suggests distance, even a certain condescendence. I often act with pity. I give some money to a beggar on the streets of Toronto or New York City, but I do not look him in his eyes, sit down with him, or talk with him. I am too busy to really pay attention to the man who reaches out to me. My money replaces my personal attention and gives me an excuse to walk on.

Compassion means to become close to the one who suffers. But we can come close to another person only when we are willing to become vulnerable ourselves. A compassionate person says: "I am your brother; I am your sister; I am human, fragile, and mortal, just like you. I am not scandalized by your tears, nor afraid of your pain. I too have wept. I too have felt pain." We can be with the other only when the other ceases to be "other" and becomes like us.

This, perhaps, is the main reason that we sometimes find it easier to show pity than compassion. The suffering person calls us to become aware of our own suffering. How can I respond to someone's loneliness unless I am in touch with my own experience of loneliness? How can I be close to handicapped people when I refuse to acknowledge my own handicaps? How can I be with the poor when I am unwilling to confess my own poverty?

When I reflect on my own life, I realize that the moments of greatest comfort and consolation were moments when someone said: "I cannot take your pain away, I cannot offer you a solution for your problem, but I can promise you that I won't leave you alone and will hold on to you as long and as well as I can." There is much grief and pain in our lives, but what a blessing it is when we do not have to live our grief and pain alone. That is the gift of compassion.

Seven: Together in Silence

Moments of true compassion will remain engraved on our hearts as long as we live. Often these are moments without words: moments of deep silence.

I remember an experience of feeling totally abandoned — my heart in anguish, my mind going crazy with despair, my body shaking wildly. I cried, screamed, and pounded the floors and the walls. Two friends were with me. They didn't say anything. They just were there. When, after several hours, I calmed down a little bit, they were still there. They put their arms around me and held me, rocking me like a little child. Then we simply sat on the floor. My friends gave me something to drink; I couldn't speak. There was silence . . . safe silence.

Today I think of that experience as a turning point in my life. I don't know how I would have survived without my friends.

I also remember the time that a friend came to me and told me that his wife had left him that day. He sat in front of me, tears streaming from his eyes. I didn't know what to say. There simply was nothing to say. My friend didn't need words. What he needed was simply to be with a friend. I held his hands in mine, and we sat there . . . silently. For a moment, I wanted to ask him how and why it all had happened, but I knew that this was not the time for questions. It was the time just to be together as friends who have nothing to say, but are not afraid to remain silent together.

Today, when I think of that day, I feel a deep gratitude that my friend had entrusted his grief to me.

These moments of compassion continue to bear fruit.

Eight: Giving and Receiving

One of the most beautiful characteristics of the compassionate life is that there is always a mutuality of giving and receiving. Everyone who has truly entered into the compassionate life will say: "I have received as much as I have given." Those who have worked with the dying in Calcutta, those who have lived among the poor in the "young towns" of Lima or the "favellas" of São Paulo, those who have dedicated themselves to AIDS patients or mentally handicapped people — they all will express deep gratitude for the gifts received from those they came to help. There is probably no clearer sign of true compassion than this mutuality of giving and receiving.

One of the most memorable times of my own life was the time I spent living with the Osco Moreno family in Pamplona Alta near Lima, Peru. Pablo and his wife, Sophia, with their three children, Johnny, Maria, and Pablito, offered me their generous hospitality, even though they were very poor. I will never forget their smiles, their affection, their playfulness — all of that in the midst of a life full of worries about how to make it for another day. I went to Peru with a deep desire to help the poor. I returned home with a deep gratitude for what I had received. Later, while teaching at Harvard Divinity School, I often felt a real homesickness for "my family." I missed the children hanging onto my arms and legs, laughing loudly and sharing their cookies and drinks with me. I missed the spontaneity, the intimacy, and the generosity with which the poor of Pamplona Alta surrounded me. They literally showered me with gifts of love. No doubt, they were happy and even proud to have this tall "Gringo Padre" with them, but whatever I gave them, it was nothing compared to what I received.

The rewards of compassion are not things to wait for. They are hidden in compassion itself. I know this for sure.

Nine: The Gift of Self-Confrontation

Sometimes a life of compassion offers a gift you are not so eager to receive: the gift of self-confrontation. The poor in Peru confronted me with my impatience and my deep-seated need for efficiency and control. The handicapped in Daybreak keep confronting me with my fear of rejection, my hunger for affirmation, and my never-decreasing search for affection.

I remember quite vividly one such moment of self-confrontation. During a lecture trip to Texas, I had bought a large cowboy hat for Raymond, one of the handicapped members of the house in which I lived. I looked forward to coming home and giving him my gift.

But when Raymond, whose needs for attention and affirmation were as boundless as my own, saw my gift he started yelling at me: "I don't need your silly gift. I have enough gifts. I have no place for them in my room. My walls are already full. You better keep your gift. I don't need it." His words opened a deep wound in me. He made me realize that I *wanted* to be his friend, but instead of spending time with him and offering him my attention, I had given him an expensive gift. Raymond's angry response to the Texan hat confronted me with my inability to enter into a personal relationship with him and develop a real friendship. The hat, instead of being seen as an expression of friendship, was seen as a substitute for it.

Obviously, all of this didn't happen consciously on my side or on Raymond's side. But when Raymond's outburst brought me to tears I realized that my tears were, most of all, tears about my own inner brokenness.

This self-confrontation too is a gift of the compassionate life. It is a gift very hard to receive, but a gift that can teach us much and help us in our own search for wholeness and holiness.

Ten: God's Heart

What does it mean to live in the world with a truly compassionate heart, a heart that remains open to all people at all times? It is very important to realize that compassion is more than sympathy or empathy. When we are asked to listen to the pains of people and empathize with their suffering, we soon reach our emotional limits. We can listen only for a short time and only to a few people. In our society we are bombarded with so much "news" about human misery that our hearts easily get numbed simply because of overload.

But God's compassionate heart does not have limits. God's heart is greater, infinitely greater, than the human heart. It is that divine heart that God wants to give to us so that we can love all people without burning out or becoming numb.

It is for this compassionate heart that we pray when we say: "A pure heart create for me, O God, put a steadfast spirit within me. Do not cast me away from your presence, nor deprive me of your holy spirit" (Psalm 51).

The Holy Spirit of God is given to us so that we can become participants in God's compassion and so reach out to all people at all times with God's heart.

Chapter IX

FAMILY

One: Leaving Father and Mother

For most of my life I have given a quite literal interpretation to Jesus' words: "Leave your father, mother, brothers, and sisters for the sake of my name." I thought about these words as a call to move away from one's family, get married, enter a monastery or convent, or go to a faraway country to do missionary work. Although I still feel encouraged and inspired by those who make such a move for the sake of Jesus' name, I am discovering, as I grow older, that there is a deeper meaning to this "leaving."

Lately I have become aware of how much our emotional life is influenced by our relationship with our parents, brothers, and sisters. Quite often this influence is so strong that, even as adults who left our parents long ago, we remain emotionally bound to them. Only recently, I realized that I still wanted to change my father, hoping that he would give me the kind of attention I desired. Recently also, I have seen how the inner lives of so many of my friends are still dominated by feelings of anger, resentment, or disillusionment arising from their family relations. Even when they have not seen their parents for a long time, yes, even when their parents have already died, they still have not truly left home.

All this is very real for those who are becoming aware that they are victims of child abuse. This discovery can suddenly bring the home situation back to mind and heart in an excruciatingly painful way.

In this context, Jesus' call to leave father and mother, brothers, and sisters, receives a whole new meaning. Are we able and willing to unhook ourselves from the restraining emotional bonds that prevent us from following our deepest vocation? This is a question with profound implications for our emotional and spiritual well-being.

Two: Free to Follow Jesus

Leaving father, mother, brothers and sisters for Jesus' sake is a lifelong task. It is only gradually that we realize how we go on clinging to the negative as well as to the positive experiences of our youth and how hard it is to leave it all and be on our own. To leave "home," whether it was a good home or a bad home, is one of the greatest spiritual challenges of our life.

I had already left my family and my country for more than twenty years when I became fully aware that I was still trying to live up to the expectations of my father and mother. In fact, I was shocked when I found out that many of my work habits, career decisions, and life choices were still deeply motivated by my desire to please my family. I still wanted to be the son or the brother they could be proud of. When I saw this in myself, I also started to see it in the lives of many of my friends. Some of them, who already had grown-up children, still suffered from the rejection they experienced from their parents. Others who carved out impressive careers and won many rewards and prizes still had deep hopes that, one day, their father or mother would acknowledge their gifts. Others again, who suffered many disappointments in their personal relations or work, still blamed their parents for their misfortunes.

The older we grow, the more we come to see the

deep roots of our ties with those who were our main guides during the formative years of our lives.

Jesus wants to set us free, free from everything that prevents us from fully following our vocation, free also from everyone who prevents us from fully knowing God's unconditional love. To come to that freedom we have to keep leaving our fathers, mothers, brothers, and sisters, and dare to follow him . . . even there where we rather would not go.

Three: Forgiveness and Gratitude

Two of the most important ways of leaving father, mother, brother, and sister are forgiveness and gratitude. Can we forgive our family for not having loved us as well as we wanted to be loved? Can we forgive our fathers for being demanding, authoritarian, indifferent, unaffectionate, absent, or simply more interested in other people or things than in us? Can we forgive our mothers for being possessive, scrupulous, controlling, preoccupied, addicted to food, alcohol, or drugs, overly busy, or simply more concerned with a career than with us? Can we forgive our brothers and sisters for not playing with us, for not sharing their friends with us, for talking down to us, or for making us feel stupid or useless?

There is a lot to forgive, not just because our family was not as caring as other families, but because all the love we received was imperfect and very limited. Our parents also are children of parents who didn't love them in a perfect way, and even our grandparents had parents who were not ideal!

There is so much to forgive. But if we are willing to see our own parents, grandparents, and great-grandparents as people like ourselves with a desire to love but also with many unfulfilled needs, we might be able to step over our anger, our resentments, or even our hatred, and discover that their limited love is still real love, a love for which to be grateful.

Once we are able to forgive, we can be grateful for what we have received. And we have received so much. We can walk, talk, smile, move, laugh, cry, eat, drink, dance, play, work, sing, give life, give joy, give hope, give love. We are alive! Our fathers and mothers gave us life, and our brothers and sisters helped us to live it. Once we are no longer blinded by their so-obvious weaknesses, we can see clearly how much there is to be grateful for.

Four: Many Mothers and Fathers

In the Broadway play *Conversations with My Father,* a famous author lives his life with the hope that, one day, his father, who runs a little bar in New York City, will read his work and praise him for it. But it doesn't happen. Instead, the father says to his son: "I am only Ed, I don't read books, just let me be Ed." The son finally realizes that *he* is the one that has to change and love his father as he is. Thus they can become brothers.

One of the most beautiful things that can happen in a human life is that parents become brothers and sisters for their children, that children become fathers and mothers for their parents, that brothers and sisters become friends and that fatherhood, motherhood, brotherhood, and sisterhood are deeply shared by all the members of the family at different times and on different occasions.

But this cannot happen without leaving. Only to the degree that we have broken the ties that keep us captives of an imperfect love can we be free to love those we have left as father, mother, brother, or sister and receive their love in the same way. This is what Jesus means when he says: "In truth I tell you, there is no one who has left house, brothers, sisters, mother, father, children, or land for my sake and for the sake of the gospel, who will not receive a hundred times as much houses, brothers, sisters, mothers, children, and land — and persecutions too — now in this present time and, in the world to come, eternal life" (Mark 10:29–30).

The great mystery of leaving father and mother is, indeed, that their limited love will multiply and manifest itself wherever we go, because only insofar as we leave, can the love we clung to reveal its true source.

Five: To Be Forgiven

Many of us not only *have* parents but also *are* parents. This simple truth is quite sobering because it is not unlikely that our own children will spend quite a lot of time talking to their friends, counselors, psychiatrists, and priests about us! And we tried so hard not to make the same mistakes our parents made! Still, it is quite possible that, while we may be more tolerant than our fathers or mothers, our children may be complaining that we weren't strict enough!

And it is not unthinkable that, while we were making sure that our children were free to choose their own lifestyle, religion, or career, they may be talking about us as weak characters not daring to give concrete directions!

The tragedy of our lives is that, while we suffer from the wounds afflicted on us by those who love us, we cannot avoid wounding those we want to love. We so much want to love well, to care well, to understand well, but before we grow old someone will say to us "You weren't there for me when I most needed you; you didn't care about what I was doing or thinking; you didn't understand or even try to understand me." As we hear these remarks or feel the criticisms of those we love, we come to the painful realization that — as we had to leave our father and mother, brothers and sisters — they too have to leave us to find their own freedom. It is very painful to see those for whom we have given our life leave us, often in directions that fill us with fear.

It is here that we are called to believe deeply in the truth that all fatherhood and all motherhood come from God. Only God is the father and mother who can love us as we need and want to be loved.

This belief, when strongly held, can free us, not only to forgive our parents, but also to let our children forgive us.

Six: Children Are Gifts

Being a parent is like being a good host to a stranger! While we may think that our children are like us, we are continually surprised at how different they are. We can be gladdened by their intelligence, their artistic gifts, or their athletic prowess, or saddened by their slowness in learning, their lack of coordination, or their "odd" interests. In many ways we don't know our children.

We didn't create our own children, nor do we own them. This is good news. We don't need to blame ourselves for all their problems, nor should we claim for ourselves their successes.

Children are gifts from God. They are given to us so that we can offer them a safe, loving place to grow to inner and outer freedom. They are like strangers who ask for hospitality, become good friends, and then leave again to continue their journey. They bring immense joy and immense sorrow precisely because they are gifts. And a good gift, as a proverb says, is "twice given." The gift we receive, we have to give again. When our child leaves us to study, to look for work, to marry, to join a community, or simply to become independent, sorrow and joy touch each other. Because it is then that we feel deeply that "our" child isn't really "ours" but given to us to become a true gift for others.

It is so hard to give our children their freedom — especially in this violent and exploitative world. We so much want to protect them from all possible dangers. But we cannot. They do not belong to us. They belong to God, and one of the greatest acts of trust in God is letting our children make their own choices and find their own way.

Seven: The Pain of Love

Our greatest pain often comes from our inability to help others — especially those we love so much. A close friend of mine had been looking forward to sending his son to college after graduation from high school. He had helped him look at the different schools and was eagerly awaiting his choice.

But when the graduation had come and gone, the son came home with a "fuzzy-looking" girl in an old red convertible and told his father that he was going to travel west with his girl, sleeping by the roadside, and looking for work whenever they ran out of money.

My friend could imagine only drugs, sex, and craziness and feared for the very life of his son. Rightly so. But all his pleading and warning only strengthened his son's resolve to escape his "bourgeois" milieu and explore the "real world."

It was a very scary situation, and my friend's fear was far from imaginary. Still, the final question was not: "How to help this unruly teenager?" but "How to prevent the father from being destroyed by his son?" I kept saying to him: "Whatever happens to your son, you cannot allow him to take away your sleep, your appetite, and all your joy. You must claim your own talents and gifts as a man, and, more than ever before, live a life that is fully yours." It wasn't easy for me to say these things because I shared my friend's worries. But painful as his son's leaving was, he had to let him leave, not just physically, but emotionally as well. In this way, if the son would return, he would find a healthy father at home.

Eight: Our Worrying Minds

People often say: "Don't worry, things will work out fine." But we *do* worry and we can't stop worrying just because someone tells us to. One of the painful things of life is that we worry a great deal about our children, our friends, our spouse, our job, our future, our family, our country, our world, and endless other things. We know the answer to Jesus' question: "Can any of you, however much you worry, add one single cubit to your span of life?" (Matthew 6:27). We know that our worrying does not help us nor does it solve any of our problems. Still, we worry a lot and, therefore, suffer a lot. We wish that we could stop worrying, but we don't know how. Even though we realize that, tomorrow, we may have forgotten what we were worrying about so much today, we still find it impossible to turn off our anxious minds.

My mother, who was a very caring and prayerful woman, worried a lot, especially about me and my brothers and sister. When I spent time at home she could never go to sleep until she was sure I had safely returned to the house. This was the case, not only when I was a teenager and liked to hang out with my friends late at night, but also after I had traveled far and wide by plane, train, and bus and had been in quite dangerous situations. Whenever I came home, whether I was eighteen or forty years old, my mother would stay awake worrying about her child until she was sure that he was safely in bed!

Most of us are not very different. So the real question is: Can we do anything to worry less and be more at peace? If it is true that we cannot change anything by worrying about it, how then can we train our hearts and minds not to waste time and energy with anxious ruminations that make us spin around inside of ourselves. Jesus says: "Set your heart on God's kingdom first." That gives us a hint as to the right direction.

Chapter X

RELATIONSHIPS

One: Complexity of Intimacy

To love is hard work! In our society, love is sung, written, and spoken about as a beautiful ideal we all desire. But while Madonna sings her love songs and one movie after the other allows us to witness the most intimate ways of love-making, the day-to-day reality is that most friendships do not last long, that many lovers can't hold on to each other, that countless marriages go sour or break up, and that numerous communities go from crisis to crisis. There is an immense fragmentation in human relationships. While the desire for love has seldom been so directly expressed, love in its daily appearance has seldom looked so broken. While in our intensely competitive society the hunger and thirst for friendship, intimacy, union, and communion are immense, it never has been so difficult to satisfy this hunger and quench this thirst.

The word that is central in it all is "relationship."

We desire to break out of our isolation and loneliness and enter into a relationship that offers us a sense of home, an experience of belonging, a feeling of safety, and a sense of being well connected. But every time we explore such a relationship, we discover quickly the difficulty of being close to anybody and the complexity of intimacy between people.

When we are lonely and look for someone to take our loneliness away, we are quickly disillusioned. The other, who for a while may have offered us an experience of wholeness and inner peace, soon proves incapable of giving us lasting happiness and instead of taking away our loneliness only reveals to us its depth. The stronger our expectation that another human being will fulfill our deepest desires, the greater the pain is when we are confronted with the limitations of human relationships. And our need for intimacy easily turns into a demand. But as soon as we start demanding love from another person, love turns into violence, caressing becomes hitting, kissing becomes biting, looking tenderly becomes looking suspiciously, hearing becomes overhearing, and sexual intercourse becomes rape.

Seeing the intense need for love and the frightening explosion of violence so closely connected in our society, we are faced with the crucial question: What is the hard work of love?

Two: To Be Called Together

What does it mean to love another person? Mutual affection, intellectual compatibility, sexual attraction, shared ideals, a common financial, cultural, and religious background, all of these can be important factors for a good relationship, but they do not guarantee love.

I once met a young man and woman who wanted to get married. Both were very good looking, very intelligent, very similar in family background, and very much in love with each other. They had spent many hours with qualified psychotherapists to explore their psychological pasts and to face directly their emotional strengths and weaknesses. In every respect they seemed well prepared to get married and have a happy life together.

Still, the question remains: Will these two people be able to love each other well, not just for a while or a few years, but for a lifetime? For me, who was asked to accompany these two people, this was not as obvious as it was to them. They had been facing each other for a long time and became secure in their feelings of love for each other, but would they be able to face together a world in which there is so little support for a lasting relationship? Where would the strength come from to remain faithful to one another in times of conflict, economic pressure, deep grief, illness, and necessary separations? What would it mean for this man and this woman to love one another as husband and wife until death?

The more I reflected on this, the more I felt that marriage is foremost a vocation. Two people are called together to fulfill the mission that God has given them. Marriage is a spiritual reality. That is to say, a man and a woman come together for life, not just because they experience deep love for each other, but because they believe that God loves each of them with an infinite love and has called them to each other to be living witnesses of that love. To love is to embody God's infinite love in a faithful communion with another human being.

Three: Living Witnesses of God's Love

All human relationships, be they between parents and children, husbands and wives, lovers and friends, or between members of a community, are meant to be signs of God's love for humanity as a whole and each person in particular. This is a very uncommon viewpoint, but it is the viewpoint of Jesus. Jesus says: "You must love one another just as I have loved you. It is by your love for one another that everyone will recognize you as my disciples" (John 13:34–35). And how does Jesus love us? He says: "I have loved you, just as the Father has loved me" (John 15:9). Jesus' love for us is the full expression of God's love for us, because Jesus and the Father are one. "What I say to you," Jesus says, "I do not speak of my own accord: it is the Father, living in me, who is doing his works. You must believe me when I say that I am in the Father and the Father is in me" (John 14:10–11).

These words may at first sound very unreal and mystifying, but they have a direct and radical implication for how we live our relationships on a day-to-day basis.

Jesus reveals to us that we are called by God to be living witnesses of God's love. We become such witnesses by following Jesus and loving one another as he loves us. What does this say about marriage, friendship, and community? It says that the source of the love that sustains these relationships is not the partners themselves but God who calls the partners together. Loving one another is not clinging to one another so as to be safe in a hostile world, but living together in such a way that everyone will recognize us as people who make God's love visible to the world. Not only does all fatherhood and motherhood come from God, but also all friendship, partnership in marriage, and true intimacy and community. When we live as if human relationships are "human-made" and therefore subject to the shifting and changing of human regulations and customs, we cannot expect anything but the immense fragmentation and alienation that characterize our society. But when we claim and constantly reclaim God as the source of all love, we will discover love as God's gift to God's people.

Four: Revealing God's Faithfulness

To be truthful all human relationships must find their source in God and witness to God's love. One of the most important qualities of God's love is faithfulness. God is a faithful God, a God who fulfills the divine promise and will never let us down. God shows this faithfulness to Abraham and Sarah, Isaac and Rebecca, Jacob and Rachel. God shows this faithfulness to Moses and Aaron and to the people as they move from Egypt to the promised land. But God's faithfulness goes beyond that. God wants not only to be a God *for* us, but also a God *with* us. That happens in Jesus, the Emmanuel who walks with us, talks with us, and dies with us. In sending Jesus to us, God wants to convince us of the unshakeable fidelity of the divine love.

Still there is more. When Jesus leaves he says to us, "I will not leave you alone, but will send you the Holy Spirit." The Spirit of Jesus is God *within* us. Here the fullness of God's faithfulness is revealed. Through Jesus, God gives us the divine Spirit so that we can live a God-like life. The Spirit is the breath of God. It is the intimacy between Jesus and his Father.

It is the divine communion. It is God's love active within us.

This divine faithfulness is the core of our witness. By our words, but most of all by our lives, we are to reveal God's faithfulness to the world. The world is not interested in faithfulness, because faithfulness does not help in the acquisition of success, popularity, and power. But when Jesus calls us to love one another as he has loved us, he calls us to faithful relationships, not based on the pragmatic concerns of the world, but on the knowledge of God's everlasting love.

Faithfulness, obviously, does not mean sticking it out together to the bitter end. That is no reflection of God's love. Faithfulness means that every decision we make in our lives together is guided by the deep awareness that we are called to be living signs of God's faithful presence among us. And this requires an attentiveness to one another that goes far beyond any formal obligation.

Five: Living Discipleship Together

Marriage is one way to be a living witness to God's faithful love. Once a man and a woman decide to live their married life in this way, their relationship takes on a radically new meaning. Their love for each other, whatever its emotional content, becomes an expression of their discipleship of Jesus; therefore, their main concern is to live that discipleship as a couple.

For many people discipleship is an individual or even private affair. They say: "Religion is my own business. I don't want to be bothered by others in the practice of my religion, and I won't bother anyone else in theirs." This attitude even enters into the intimacy of marriage. A man says: "My wife's religion is her private affair." A woman says: "I leave my husband completely free when it comes to his religion." But this is not living discipleship together. Marriage looked upon from above is God creating a new communion between two people, so that through that visible and tangible communion a new sign will be present in the world to point people toward God's love.

When two people commit themselves to live their lives together, a new reality comes into existence. "They become one flesh," Jesus says. That means that their unity creates a new sacred place. Many relationships are like interlocking fingers. Two people cling to each other as two hands interlocked in fear. They connect because they cannot survive individually. But as they interlock they also realize that they cannot take away each other's loneliness. And it is then that friction arises and tension increases. Often a breakup is the final result.

But God calls man and woman into a different relationship. It is a relationship that looks like two hands that fold in an act of prayer. The fingertips touch, but the hands can create a space, like a little tent. Such a space is the space created by love, not by fear. Marriage is creating a new, open space where God's love can be revealed to the "stranger": the child, the friend, the visitor.

This marriage becomes a witness to God's desire to be among us as a faithful friend.

Six: Choosing Our Friends

The spiritual life is one of constant choices. One of the most important choices is the choice of the people with whom we develop close intimate relationships. We have only a limited amount of time in our lives.

With whom do we spend it and how? That's probably one of the most decisive questions of our lives. It is not without reason that parents are very concerned about who their children bring home as playmates, friends, or lovers. They know that much of their children's happiness will depend on those they choose to be close to.

To whom do we go for advice? With whom do we spend our free evenings? With whom are we going on vacation? Sometimes we speak or act as if we have little choice in the matter. Sometimes we act as though we will be lucky if there is anyone who wants to be our friend. But that is a very passive and even fatalistic attitude. If we truly believe that God loves us with an unlimited, unconditional love, then we can trust that there are women and men in this world who are eager to show us that love. But we cannot wait passively until someone shows up to offer us friendship. As people who trust in God's love, we must have the courage and the confidence to say to someone through whom God's love becomes visible to us: "I would like to get to know you, I would like to spend time with you. I would like to develop a friendship with you. What about you?"

There will be no's, there will be the pain of rejection. But when we determine to avoid all no's and all rejections, we will never create the milieu where we can grow stronger and deepen in love. God became human for us to make divine love tangible. That is what incarnation is all about. That incarnation not only happened long ago, but it continues to happen for those who trust that God will give us the friends we need. But the choice is ours!

Chapter XI

WHO WE ARE

One: We Are God's Beloved Children

During our short lives the question that guides much of our behavior is: "Who are we?" Although we may seldom pose that question in a formal way, we live it very concretely in our day-to-day decisions.

The three answers that we generally live — not necessarily give — are: "We are what we do, we are what others say about us, and we are what we have," or in other words: "We are our success, we are our popularity, we are our power."

It is important to realize the fragility of life that depends on success, popularity, and power. Its fragility stems from the fact that all three of these are external factors over which we have only limited control. Losing our job, our fame, or our wealth often is caused by events completely beyond our control. But when we depend on them, we have sold ourselves to the world, because then we *are* what the world gives us. Death takes it all away from us. The final statement then becomes: "When we are dead, we are dead!" because when we die, we can't do anything anymore, people don't talk about us anymore, and we have nothing anymore. When we *are* what the world makes us, we can't *be* after we have left the world.

Jesus came to announce to us that an identity based on success, popularity, and power is a false identity — an illusion! Loudly and clearly he says: "You are not what the world makes you; but you are children of God."

Two: Claiming Our Belovedness

The spiritual life requires a constant claiming of our true identity. Our true identity is that we are God's children, the beloved sons and daughters of our heavenly Father. Jesus' life reveals to us this mysterious truth. After Jesus was baptized in the Jordan by John, as he was coming up out of the water, he saw the heavens torn apart and the Spirit, like a dove, descending on him. And a voice came from heaven: "You are my Son, the Beloved; my favor rests on you" (Mark 1:10–11). This is the decisive moment of Jesus' life. His true identity is declared to him. He is the Beloved of God. As "the Beloved" he is being sent into the world so that through him all people will discover and claim their own belovedness.

But the same Spirit who descended on Jesus and affirmed his identity as the Beloved Son of God also drove him into the desert to be tested by Satan. Satan asked him to prove his belovedness by changing stones to bread, by throwing himself from the temple tower to be carried by angels, and by accepting the kingdoms of the world. But Jesus resisted these temptations of success, popularity, and power by claiming strongly for himself his true identity. Jesus didn't have to prove to the world that he was worthy of love. He already was the "Beloved," and this Belovedness allowed him to live free from the manipulative games of the world, always faithful to the voice that had spoken to him at the Jordan. Jesus' whole life was a life of obedience, of attentive listening to the One who called him the Beloved. Everything that Jesus said or did came forth from that most intimate spiritual communion. Jesus' revealed to us that we sinful, broken human beings are invited to that same communion that Jesus lived, that we are the beloved sons and daughters of God just as he is the Beloved Son, that we are sent into the world to proclaim the belovedness of all people as he was and that we will finally escape the destructive powers of death as he did.

Three: The Discipline of Prayer

One of the tragedies of our life is that we keep forgetting who we are and waste a lot of time and energy to prove what doesn't need to be proved. We are God's beloved daughters and sons, not because we have proven ourselves worthy of God's love, but because God freely chose us. It is very hard to stay in touch with our true identity because those who want our money, our time, and our energy profit more from our insecurity and fears than from our inner freedom.

We, therefore, need discipline to keep living truthfully and not succumb to the endless seductions of our society. Wherever we are there are voices saying: "Go here, go there, buy this, buy that, get to know him, get to know her, don't miss this, don't miss that," and so on and on. These voices keep pulling us away from that soft gentle voice that speaks in the center of our being: "You are my beloved, on you my favor rests."

Prayer is the discipline of listening to that voice of love. Jesus spent many nights in prayer listening to the voice that had spoken to him at the Jordan River. We too must pray. Without prayer, we become deaf to the voice of love and become confused by the many competing voices asking for our attention. How difficult this is! When we sit down for half an hour — without talking to someone, listening to music, watching television, or reading a book — and try to become very still, we often find ourselves so overwhelmed by our noisy inner voices that we can hardly wait to get busy and distracted again. Our inner life often looks like a banana tree full of jumping monkeys! But when we decide not to run away and stay focused, these monkeys may gradually go away because of lack of attention, and the soft gentle voice calling us the beloved may gradually make itself heard. Much of Jesus' prayer took place during the night. "Night" means more than the absence of the sun. It also means the absence of satisfying feelings or enlightening insights. That's why it is so hard to be faithful. But God is greater than our hearts and minds and keeps calling us the beloved . . . far beyond all feelings and thoughts.

Four: No Victims of Clock-Time

Each time we claim for ourselves the truth of our belovedness, our lives are widened and deepened. As the beloved our lives stretch out far beyond the boundaries of our birth and death. We do not simply become the beloved at our birth and cease being the beloved at our death. Our belovedness is eternal. God says to us: "I love you with an everlasting love." This love was there before our fathers and mothers loved us, and it will be there long after our friends have cared for us. It is a divine love, an everlasting love, an eternal love.

Precisely because our true identity is rooted in this unconditional, unlimited, everlasting love, we can escape being victimized by our "clock-time." Clock-time is the time we have in this world. That time can be measured in seconds, minutes, hours, days, weeks, months, and years. Our clock-time, *chronos* in Greek, can become an obsession, especially when

167

all that we are is connected with the clock that keeps ticking whether we are awake or asleep.

I have always been very conscious of my clock-time. Often I asked myself: "Can I still double my years?" When I was thirty I said: "I can easily live another thirty!" When I was forty, I mused, "Maybe I am only halfway!" Today I can no longer say that, and my question has become: "How am I going to use the few years left to me?" All these concerns about our clock-time come from below. They are based on the presupposition that our chronology is all we have to live. But looked upon from above, from God's perspective, our clock-time is embedded in the timeless embrace of God. Looked upon from above, our years on earth are not simply *chronos* but *kairos* — another Greek word for time — which is the opportunity to claim for ourselves the love that God offers us from eternity to eternity. And so our short lives, instead of being that limited amount of years to which we must anxiously cling, become that saving opportunity to respond with all of our hearts, souls, and minds to God's love and so become true partners in the divine communion.

Five: Preparing for Death

Some people say they are afraid of death. Others say they are not. But most people are quite afraid of dying. The slow deterioration of mind and body, the pains of a growing cancer, the ravaging effects of AIDS, becoming a burden for your friends, losing control of your movements, being talked about or spoken to with half-truths, forgetting recent events and the names of visitors — all of that and much more is what we really fear. It's not surprising that we sometimes say: "I hope it doesn't last long. I hope I will die through a sudden heart attack and not after a long, painful illness."

But, whatever we think or hope, the way we will die is unpredictable and our worries about it quite fruitless. Still we need to be prepared. Preparing ourselves for death is the most important task of life, at least when we believe that death is not the total dissolution of our identity but the way to its fullest revelation. Death, as Jesus speaks about it, is that moment in which total defeat and total victory are one. The cross on which Jesus died is the sign of this oneness of defeat and victory. Jesus speaks about his

169

death as being "lifted up." Lifted up on the cross as well as lifted up in the resurrection. Jesus wants our death to be like his, a death in which the world banishes us but God welcomes us home.

How, then, do we prepare ourselves for death? By living each day in the full awareness of being children of God, whose love is stronger than death. Speculations and concerns about the final days of our life are useless, but making each day into a celebration of our belovedness as sons and daughters of God will allow us to live our final days, whether short or long, as birthing days. The pains of dying are labor pains. Through them, we leave the womb of this world and are born to the fullness of children of God.

John says it clearly: "My dear friends, you must see what great love the Father has lavished on us by letting us be called God's children — which is what we are! — we are already God's children, but what we shall be in the future has not yet been revealed. We are well aware that when he appears we shall be like him, because we shall see him as he really is" (1 John 3:1–2).

By claiming what we already are, we best prepare ourselves for what we shall be.

Six: Going Home

Our life is a short opportunity to say "yes" to God's love. Our death is a full coming home to that love. Do we desire to come home? It seems that most of our efforts are aimed at delaying this homecoming as long as possible.

Writing to the Christians at Philippi, the apostle Paul shows a radically different attitude. He says: "I want to be gone and be with Christ, and this is by far the stronger desire — and yet for your sake to stay alive in this body is a more urgent need." Paul's deepest desire is to be completely united with God through Christ and that desire makes him look at death as a "positive gain." His other desire, however, is to stay alive in the body and fulfill his mission. That will offer him an opportunity for fruitful work.

We are challenged once again to look at our lives from above. When, indeed, Jesus came to offer us full communion with God, by making us partakers of his death and resurrection, what else can we desire but to leave our mortal bodies and so reach the final goal of our existence? The only reason for staying in this valley of tears can be to continue the mission of Jesus who has sent us into the world as his Father sent him into the world. Looking from above, life is a short, often painful mission, full of occasions to do fruitful work for God's kingdom, and death is the open door that leads into the hall of celebration where the king himself will serve us.

It all seems such an upside-down way of being! But it's the way of Jesus and the way for us to follow. There is nothing morbid about it. To the contrary, it's a joyful vision of life and death. As long as we are in the body, let us care well for our bodies so that we can bring the joy and peace of God's kingdom to those we meet on our journey. But when the time has come for our dying and death let us rejoice that we can go home and be united with the One who calls us the beloved.

Afterword

One of the main experiences in writing these meditations was that in the writing I discovered how much more there is to write. Therefore this afterword is very artificial. It could as well be a foreword to many more meditations. But I am glad with this "open ending," because it encourages me to enter ever more deeply into the divine mystery with the knowledge that this mystery is an inexhaustible source of life and love. I know that there is so much more to write about the spiritual life, each word asking for a new word, each book asking for a new book.

To you who have read some or all of these meditations I want to say: Do not stop here. Continue on your own. My words were only to encourage you to find your own words, and my thoughts were only to help you discover your own thoughts. What I have written in this book is an expression of my own personal spiritual journey, bound by my own personality, time, place, and circumstances. Your spiritual journey is as unique as mine; it has its own unique beauty and unique boundaries.

My hope is that the description of God's love in *my* life will give you the freedom and the courage to discover — and maybe also describe — God's love in *yours.*

Guide for Reflection

These reflections may be used for personal meditation or in small groups.

Chapter I: A New Beginning

1. "A new beginning! We must learn to live each day, each hour, yes, each minute as a new beginning, as a unique opportunity to make everything new" (p. 16). Try to imagine what your life would be like if you began to live in the moment. How does this challenge and excite you?

2. "The world of the past has gone" (Revelation 21:4, p. 17). When you think about your past, what images and memories are strongest for you? Do you think of family, career, or friends? Do you remember most vividly the pleasant memories or the times when you wish you had done things differently?

    Write down three memories of great pain from your past. Write down three preoccupations ("what ifs") you feel about the future.

3. "God is a God of the present. God is always in the moment, be that moment hard or easy, joyful or painful" (p. 18). Look at your responses above. When you think of them, what do you imagine God would say about them? Do you think of God as keeping a record of flaws and mistakes? What does Nouwen suggest about God's presence? ("Jesus came to wipe away the burden of the past and the worries for the future," p. 19.)

4. "To celebrate a birthday means to say to someone: 'Thank you for being you' " (p. 19). How often do you or the people you know celebrate birthdays? When is the last time you celebrated someone simply for being who they are?

   Reflect on your attitude when celebrating your or another's birthday and see how you can deepen your gratitude for your own or someone else's life. You may want to call, write, or e-mail a relative or friend in the coming days to tell them of your gratitude.

5. "It is not easy to remain focused on the present. Our mind is hard to master and keeps pulling us away from the moment" (p. 21). Take five or ten minutes to close your eyes and pray or meditate, asking God to help you listen. What thoughts do you become aware of? What anxieties? How might your awareness of these distractions help you become a better listener?

6. "Take a simple prayer, a sentence or a word, and slowly repeat it" (p. 22). In the coming days, waiting

at a stoplight or in line at the supermarket or bank, repeat a phrase or simple prayer. (Example: "God of love, come to me.") Don't worry about choosing the "right" words. What matters is that you choose a word or phrase and repeat it whenever you can.

7. "We are children of one God" (p. 25). Keep these words in mind over the next several days. Repeat them when you look in the mirror, and repeat them to yourself when you encounter others, whether you know them or not.

Chapter II: Joy

1. "We have to choose joy and keep choosing it every day" (p. 29). Have you ever set aside time in your day to "choose joy"? Take a few minutes now to think what it means to choose joy, and then try doing this for the rest of your day. What does joy mean in your life right now?

2. "Maybe we could spend a moment at the end of each day and decide to remember that day — whatever may have happened — as a day to be grateful for" (p. 30). Using Nouwen's words as a guide, set aside time for the next seven nights to reflect on each day and view it as something to be grateful for. How does this perspective help you view the "sad" parts of each day in a different way?

3. "I have a friend who radiates joy" (p. 31). Have you ever known someone who radiated joy? What was it about them that showed the joy in their hearts? Where in your heart do you find your own joy? Can you visit that place in your heart more often?

4. "What if the child reveals to us what is really real?" (p. 34). Think about joyful children you've known. In your opinion, what is it about them that makes them able to find joy in life? Do you have a "child" in you that wants to express joy?

5. "That's why Jesus calls us to be like children" (p. 36). How does Jesus' call challenge you to be more like a child?

6. "Hope frees us from the need to predict the future and allows us to live in the present" (p. 37). We often talk about "hope" in terms of specific things we want to happen: "I hope I get a raise in salary"; "I hope my aunt will recover from her illness." How is this kind of hope different from the hope Nouwen describes?

7. "You are my only hope, you are the source of my joy" (p. 40). Try repeating this as a prayer many times each day during the next few days.

Chapter III: Suffering

1. "The cross is a symbol of death *and* of life, of suffering *and* of joy, of defeat *and* of victory. It's the cross

that shows us the way" (p. 43). Describe in your own words how the cross symbolizes both death and life, defeat and victory.

2. "The tears of grief and the tears of joy shouldn't be too far apart" (p. 45). Have you ever lost someone close to you? How did their death affect you? After grieving over their death, have you been able to go back and celebrate their life? In what way?

3. "Why didn't you tell me, why did you keep it secret so long?" (p. 46). Think about how you would feel if close friends suffered without telling you about it. Would you wish they had let you assist them in some way? With whom have you shared your own suffering? Are there others you should tell about it? Try to act on this in the next few days.

4. "We do not like to be dependent on others" (p. 47). Think of a time when you tried to face a difficult problem on your own. If you succeeded, did you feel much satisfaction when the problem was solved?

5. "Our desire for communion will be fulfilled by the One who gave us that desire" (p. 50). Nouwen reminds us that our yearning to be with others is a gift from God. Why don't we always experience it as a "gift"? Think of times when it felt more like a struggle or burden. Can you imagine how, even when we don't achieve the communion we hope for, we can still experience the yearning as a blessing?

6. "Those who gave us much, at times asked much in return. Those who protected us also wanted to possess us at critical moments" (p. 51). Reflect on Nouwen's words for your own life. Have you ever looked back on someone who loved you and realized the "wounding" part of their love — manipulation, demands, control? How did you feel about their motives and the quality of their love? After first realizing this, were you able to go back and appreciate the positive side of their love?

   What can the imperfect love of the people closest to us tell us about God's perfect love?

7. "More important than ever is to be very faithful to my vocation to do well the few things I am called to do" (p. 53). Recall a time recently when you wished you could "do more" to help those who suffer. How can your desire to alleviate suffering everywhere help you find greater focus in your specific vocation?

Chapter IV: Conversion

1. "Ten years ago I didn't have the faintest idea that I would end up where I now am" (p. 58). Think back to your life five or ten years ago. What did you imagine your life, career, and relationships would look like? Did things work out the way you expected?

2. "From God's place, we often look like one who tries to open the locked doors of a room" (p. 60).

Have you ever been so consumed by anxiety that you felt "closed in"? Were there open doors you simply didn't notice amid your worry? How could prayer, looking at the situation "from above," have helped you discover the open door?

3. "My gay brothers are dying so that I may turn more radically to God" (p. 65). Nouwen suggests that great suffering is always a call for us to repent in our own lives. Can you think of examples in your life when you paid so much attention to suffering of the world "out there" that you ignored your own heart and your relation to God?

4. "Those whom the world has made into victims God has chosen to be bearers of good news" (p. 67). At one time or another, many people have secretly believed that someone who suffered a terrible misfortune "deserved it" or "had it coming." Can you recall an example of this way of thinking in your own life? How do Nouwen's words invite us to look at the situation differently?

5. "Imagine having no need at all to judge anybody. Imagine having no desire to decide whether someone is a good or bad person" (p. 69). Reflect on this sentence, substituting in place of the words "anybody" and "someone" the name of the person who challenges or distresses you most.

    Think of various ways — in conversations, in solitary reflection — that you have judged the morality of others. Did doing this make you feel heavier or lighter? If you have ever felt morally superior to someone else, did that give you a feeling of genuine joy?

6. "When we have become completely free from the need to judge others, we will also become completely free from the fear of being judged" (p. 72). Imagine that you feel God's love so deeply, you know that God does not judge you. Hold onto that feeling for a moment. How can the awareness of God's love, and freedom from being judged, free you from needing to judge others?

Chapter V: Disciplined Living

1. "Do we have a clear goal in life?" (p. 76). Do you have a sense of your "mission" in life? Do you ever write down or talk about the main goals for your life? What are they? (Write some of them down.) How would your life have to change to make "eternal life" one of your goals?

2. "When eternal life is our clear goal it is not a distant goal. It is a goal that can be reached in the present moment" (p. 79). Nouwen shows that eternal life can be attained here and now. How is this kind of goal different from the goals that you listed above?

3. "Is there a book we are presently reading, a book that we have selected because it nurtures our mind and brings us closer to God?" (p. 81). Think of a book you have enjoyed for both the pleasure it gave you and its spiritual nourishment. Could you make reading it part of your daily life? How might you read it in a way that opens your eyes to God's spirit?

4. "The issue is not what we read, but how we read it" (pp. 82–83). Do you find yourself reading more from curiosity than from your search for truth? What will help you slow down and savor the words?

Chapter VI: The Spiritual Life

1. "As I stood at that busy intersection, I wished I were able to overhear the inner ruminations of all these people. But I soon realized that I didn't have to be so curious. My own restlessness was probably not very different from that of all those around me!" (p. 87). In a reflective moment, examine the concerns that preoccupy you. Ask yourself if they are worth your time and energy. Then think about your deepest needs and hopes — concerns that are worth your energy — and make them into a prayer.

2. "Do you love me?" (p. 88). Note the times when you have experienced that you are loved by a person. Try to put yourself in God's presence and hear in your heart God's loving words to you alone.

3. "If your faith were the size of a mustard seed, you could say to this mountain, move from here to there and it would move" (Matthew 17:19–20, p. 91). When you read these words of Jesus, do you read them as a figure of speech or as literally true? Believe for a moment that true faith can make all things possible. What would give you enough courage to ask for a miracle in your life?

4. "It is so hard to keep looking at life from above, from God's place" (p. 91) Think of a time when it seemed impossible to look at life "from above" and imagine God's purpose for some tragedy. With the passing of time, is it any easier to believe that "even the bad didn't happen outside the loving presence of God"?

5. "Together, indeed, we can be as cunning as snakes and as innocent as doves" (p. 99). Write down three or four of the most difficult things you have had to endure alone lately. How might these events be transformed if you "traveled" with others, involving them in your work and life?

Chapter VII: Prayer

1. "Worry about the things of God: truth, life, and light!" (p. 104). Reflect on the paradox Nouwen mentions: when we worry about (focus our attention on) the things above, we stop worrying altogether. Have you ever experienced this in your prayer life?

2. "The truth, however, is that a prayer, prayed from the heart, heals" (p. 106). Refer back to the prayer you chose for yourself in chapter 1 of this reflection guide. Have you used it for daily reflection? In what ways has it helped you heal?

3. "I am not alone when I pray these words" (p. 108). The next time you attend a religious service, notice when an important prayer such as the Lord's Prayer is being prayed. In what way are the people in that service connected to others through history who have prayed the same words?

4. "The many Gospel passages that I had been contemplating were gradually giving me new eyes and new ears to see and hear what was happening in the world" (p. 109). Try reading one chapter of the New Testament each day and allow yourself to be challenged by it.

5. "Over the years, many new pictures have appeared on my inner walls" (p. 111). Reflect on your own "inner walls." What pictures and words appear there? What images would you like to hang on your own "walls"?

6. "It is very hard to live a life of prayer in a milieu where no one prays or speaks lovingly about prayer" (p. 112). Describe the external circumstances of the places you spend the most time, such as your home, workplace, school, or hospital. Are the other people

there receptive to the idea of a loving God? If not, how could you use some of the other things Nouwen mentions — books, churches, friends — to create a supportive soil for your faith to grow?

Chapter VIII: Compassion

1. Do you ever find yourself trying to prove that you are better than others? Nouwen asks: "How is it possible to make compassion the center of our lives?" (p. 116). Answer this for your own life.

2. "Who will choose a hidden place when there is a place in the limelight?" (p. 119). Have you known someone who chose to let go of fame or high income in order to help others? What do you think inspired that person?

3. "True compassion always begins right where we are" (p. 124). Reflect on the people you know who are suffering "right where you are." How could you devote more time and attention to them by accepting "downward mobility" in your life?

4. "Moments of true compassion will remain engraved on our hearts as we live. Often these are moments without words: moments of deep silence" (p. 126). Have you ever known anyone who, by simply remaining silently present to the suffering of someone,

inspired you? Has someone helped you directly? Have you ever helped someone else in this way?

Chapter IX: Family

1. "Are we able and willing to unhook ourselves from the restraining emotional bonds that prevent us from following our deepest vocation?" (p. 135). In what ways do your memories of your family members restrict and restrain you?

2. "To leave 'home' is one of the greatest spiritual challenges of our life" (p. 136). How might you begin to "leave home" more completely? What emotional supports could give you courage?

3. "Our parents also are children of parents who didn't love them in a perfect way, and even our grandparents had parents who were not ideal!" (p. 138). Have you ever thought about your parents as people who were once the children of other parents? Reflect on what your parents may have experienced as children in an imperfect home.

4. "Many of us not only *have* parents but also *are* parents" (p. 140). If you are a parent or caregiver to children, how has raising children given you insight into the challenges your own parents faced in raising you? Has the experience allowed you to feel greater compassion for some of their mistakes?

5. "In this way, if the son would return, he would find a healthy father at home" (p. 144). When was the last time you saw someone close to you on the verge of making a poor decision likely to cause them a great deal of misery? Were you able to allow them to suffer or fail without your judgment or intervention? How can you do so in the future?

6. "We know that our worrying does not help us nor does it solve any of our problems. Still, we worry a lot and, therefore, suffer a lot" (p. 145). Think about a few things that cause you to worry and, in a loving prayer, offer them to God. Try to do this often.

Chapter X: Relationships

1. "To love is hard work!" (p. 148). Think of the romantic ideal of love portrayed in popular music and television and compare it to your lived experience. How are the ideal and the real different? What work do you choose to do so that you can be a man or woman of love?

2. "Would they be able to face together a world in which there is so little support for a lasting relationship?" (p. 151). Give some examples of the challenges that relationships face. Why do you think that the world does not provide stronger support for relationships?

3. "To be truthful all human relationships must find their source in God and witness to God's love" (p. 154). Think of a relationship you are now part of. Does it "witness to God's love"? If not, what choices do you need to make so that this relationship can do so?

4. "Marriage looked upon from above is God creating a new communion between two people" (p. 156). If you are married, do you and your spouse ever discuss your religious beliefs? Do you have shared beliefs? What can you do so that your marriage will grow to reflect the view "from above" of a new communion?

5. "God will give us the friends we need" (p. 159). Give thanks for past and present friends. Pray for your friends. Pray to become a better friend. Throughout the coming week, pray for the trust that God will bring you friends who will help you in your deepest needs.

Chapter XI: Who We Are

1. "Losing our job, our fame, or our wealth often is caused by events completely beyond our control" (p. 162). Consider ways that you identify yourself, not as God's Beloved, but as a successful or unsuccessful person. Pray to live first from your true identity as God's beloved child.

2. "Our true identity is that we are God's children, the beloved sons and daughters of our heavenly Father" (p. 163). Describe in your own words what it means to claim your belovedness. How can doing so free you from the temporary and passing identities we have in life? Pray for yourself and others that you will choose to welcome, believe, and live the truth.

3. "We are God's beloved daughters and sons, not because we have proven ourselves worthy of God's love, but because God freely chose us" (p. 165). Have you ever tried to prove to yourself or others that you were worthy of God's love? Quietly take time to rest, as God's beloved child in God's presence, accepting that God already loves you.

4. "When we sit down for half an hour and try to become very still, we often find ourselves so overwhelmed by our noisy inner voices that we can hardly wait to get busy and distracted again" (p. 166). What sorts of messages and ideas do your own noisy "inner voices" convey? What messages does God's voice convey when we choose to listen? Gather your distractions and offer them into God's loving care.

5. "Looked upon from above, from God's perspective, our clock-time is embedded in the timeless embrace of God" (p. 168). Imagine God speaking to you and calling you the "Beloved." Does this change your feeling about the regrets of the past and the hopes for the future?

6. "How, then, do we prepare ourselves for death? By living each day in the full awareness of being children of God, whose love is stronger than death" (p. 170). How are you growing to become daily more aware of how God's love is "stronger than death"?

7. "Let us rejoice that we can go home and be united with the One who calls us the beloved" (p. 172). Have you ever known someone who greeted his or her own death as an occasion for rejoicing? When you contemplate your own death, can you think of it as a celebration?

Afterword

"Do not stop here. Continue on your own" (p. 173). What ideas and questions are strongest in your mind at the end of reading this book? List five hopes you have for the next step of your spiritual life and offer them in prayer.